MEDIUMSHIP DEVELOPMENT: CONNECTING WITH SPIRIT

LEANNE THE BAREFOOT MEDIUM®

Mediumship Development: Connecting with Spirit
ISBN: 978-0-6455435-6-8
Category: Spiritual Development
First published 2019
2nd Edition published 2022
Edited by Sandra O'Neill
Cover design by Leanne, The Barefoot Medium®
Original image: Couple, Old, Mourning by Tumisu-@Pixabay

I0137175

ABOUT THE AUTHOR

Leanne, The Barefoot Medium®, from Brisbane, Australia is an empath, psychic and natural medium who reads for clients all over the world in private and large group settings. As a natural medium, she was born with her spiritual gifts and has connected with, been aware of and communicated with passed over loved ones, Spirit Guides, Angels and Archangels in Spirit since she was a young child. Leanne has had various encounters with Spirit as she was growing up, from seeing shadows and sparkling lights in her bedroom at night, feel as if there were people standing next to her, hearing Spirit walking around in her room or in the house and just knew they were watching her. Being highly sensitive and open to those in the Spirit world connecting with her, Leanne is easily able to sense, feel and see people's passed over loved ones, know how they were feeling before they passed, pick up on any physical symptoms and illnesses their experienced as well as know information and facts who their personality and their lives. She see's her role as a medium to be the line of communication between you and Spirit, to bring through evidence to reconnect you with loved ones in order to bring a sense of peace, healing and love to those on both sides. With her background in education, Leanne also loves to combine her work with Spirit with teaching and inspiring you to develop your intuition and spiritual abilities by sharing the knowledge and wisdom she has gathered along her journey as well as help people to move forward on their own path, manifest positive solutions to everyday concerns and embrace more love, trust and joy as they learn, grow and flourish in all areas of life.

Learn more about Leanne at www.thebarefootmedium.com.au

Kick off your shoes and join Leanne in the **Medium's Lounge** where she shares channeled guidance from Spirit, gifts and more to support you on your journey.

You will also be the first to receive access to new episodes of Barefoot with Spirit podcast shows, details about up-coming webinars, events and retreats as well as early release and pre-sale on her products, services and offerings.

www.thebarefootmedium.com.au

CONTENTS

INTRODUCTION

As a natural Medium, I was born with my spiritual gifts and have had many encounters and experiences with loved ones who have passed over to Spirit from a very young age. When I was younger I didn't really understand what was happening or what it was that I was feeling, seeing, hearing, smelling, tasting or knowing. I would see, hear, feel and just know that there were 'people' around and distinctly remember many nights where I would lay in bed hearing footsteps down the hallway, seeing outlines of Spirit people, sensing passed loved ones in the house, seeing shadows out of the corner of my eyes and feeling as if people were standing around me or at the foot of my bed and just know information about how they had passed over. I would often sleep with the light on so I would not see them, have the television playing all night so that I would not hearing them talking or walking around. I would also pull the blankets up over my face to protect myself from feeling their energy drawing close to me and so I would not be able to feel their emotions or physical pains.

Also as an Empath, I was frequently told as a child I was "too sensitive" to everything and everyone, whether people (living or passed over), or situations, events and certain environments. I felt and knew I was different to everyone else, I was shy, sensitive to others words, emotions and physical aliments and would often go within as a way of coping and trying to understand with I was seeing, hearing, feeling and experiencing from those in the physical and Spiritual world.

Many of my experiences in life and with Spirit were all part of helping me to understand how they communicate with me, how my intuition and abilities work as well as to stand in my strength, embrace the uniqueness of who I am and to shine my light out into the world with divine love, true compassion and empathy for others. I have learnt that my sensitivity is a gift that I am able to consciously and intentionally work with on a daily basis to connect with Spirit and loved one's who had passed over to gain clarity, information and guidance for myself and my clients to create a loving, joyful and abundant life.

Having experienced the loss of many loved ones who passed to the Spirit world from an early age, I understand the journey that grief can take us through and the opportunities it can bring to help us grow personally as a soul and spiritually. I also know first-hand the impact, healing and gifts of peace, comfort and love that come from being able to receive evidence through a medium that our loved ones are still connected to us, to be able to communicate with them and to feel their presence one more time.

I am also blessed to have spent over 10 years working in Senior Management positions and as a Lecturer and Tutor within a University in Brisbane (Australia), where I completed a Bachelor of Behavioural Sciences, Bachelor of Criminology and a Master in Education, connecting with students from all over the world. Together with attending meditation, spiritual development circles and workshops on a regular basis, this was where I gained many of the skills I needed to step more fully into my soul's calling to work with Spirit as a Medium. I remember on many occasions being able to clearly see my students' auras as they stood in front of the whiteboard to do their presentations which helped me to learn about the different information you can receive as well as the ways it can come through your senses from those in Spirit. Teaching large classes of students was also the perfect training ground for my work as a Platform Medium and Speaker, as I learnt how to hold the energy within a room, techniques for projecting your voice and engaging an audience while also delivering information, wisdom and guidance.

I have taken many journey's so far in life, some challenging and others easy, and have learnt that life is really just a continuous journey back to self, back to who we are at a soul level, back to what feels joyful and loving for us, back to love and the fullness of who we are - the light and the dark, the good and the bad, the ups and the downs, the beautiful and the ugly - back to our authentic selves. It is ALL part of the journey of discovery and to stay focused on what it is in life that is really important. The best part of the journey is having the opportunity to become the bridge between you and your loved one(s) to communicate and pass on messages and confirmations that your loved one's in Spirit continue to survive long after they leave this physical world. This I see as a privilege, honour and gift to be able to do each and every day.

This book Mediumship Development: Connecting with Spirit, provides you with easy, simple and practical techniques you can use to understand more about how to blend and communicate with loved one's who have passed to Spirit through mediumship connections. You will also learn about the difference between a psychic and mediumship sitting, gain an understanding of the different perspectives people have about death and the grieving process, how to structure a sitting as well as how you can build a stronger relationship with your Spirit Guides to support you in your mediumship development. In this book, I have included not only some of the information and wisdom I have gathered over the years, but also some very simple and easy to follow strategies to help you understand the different types of information and evidence that those in Spirit can bring through in a sitting as well as the fundamental skills necessary to be able to deliver clear accurate evidential mediumship sittings to others. For those of you who are interested in working with Spirit, I hope this book helps you to be able to step more fully into developing your mediumship abilities and to be able to experience first-hand the privilege, honour and blessing it is to be able to reconnect people with their loved ones who have passed over.

CHAPTER 1. FOUNDATIONS OF MEDIUMSHIP

It is absolutely essential before you begin working with your mediumship that you have a solid foundation and in-depth understanding of the basic principles of energy, fundamental skills and techniques for working with your intuition and spiritual awareness so that you are able to tune into, blend and communicate with those in the Spirit realms more easily. While a brief summary of the foundations you require in order to step into your mediumship has been included below, it is recommended that you read "Psychic Development: Basics of Working with Spirit" followed by "Psychic Development: Divination Tools and Techniques" for an in-depth discussion as well as practical tools and techniques to ensure you are solid before moving forward.

PSYCHIC V'S MEDIUMSHIP

Many people do not know the difference between a Psychic and a Mediumship reading, so it is important when stepping into your spiritual development to understand and be able to easily recognise and identify the difference between a psychic and mediumship connection on both a physical and spiritual level. Firstly, everyone is intuitive and psychic to some extent, however, while all mediums are psychic not all psychics are mediums and able to connect and bring through information from those in the Spirit world. Secondly, Mediums are born and often have psychic and spirit experiences, events and circumstances from early childhood that may or may not emerge fully until later in life. Finally, as you will see in more details below, a psychic reading is more about predicting the future, whereas a mediumship reading is about getting evidence and facts to prove who a Spirit communicator is beyond reasonable doubt.

PSYCHIC

A Psychic connection involves 'reading' or sensing things most people are unable to pick up and involves tuning into the energy field (aura) that surrounds 'the sitter' or person that you are reading for to gather information. During a psychic reading you are gathering information from your 'sitter' and providing insights, information and guidance about events, situations and experiences in the past, where they are currently in their journey, what is taking place in the present moment as well as the possibilities for the future, whether around love, relationships, work, career, finances, home, health and well-being and much more. Many psychic readers use various divination tools to help guide them, for example the images and/or symbols in tarot cards which can be interpreted and connected to 'the sitter' as well as additional information from their inner visions to help provide 'the sitter' with guidance. A psychic works with their basic sense of intuition and psychic abilities to gather information to ultimately help 'the sitter' to connect with their own higher self and enable them to see the path ahead more clearly. It is important to be aware that many psychic readings often focus on predicting or 'seeing' into the future, however, it is important to remember that everyone was given the gift of free-will when they came into this world and at any moment in time can redirect their course and create the life they want by changing their thoughts and actions. Psychic information is often just insight into what potentially could happen based on the road 'the sitter' is currently travelling - and it should be used only as a guideline to help the person make the best choices for themselves.

MEDIUMSHIP

A mediumship connection is essentially about blending, connecting and tuning into energy of the 'spirit world' and being a 'channel' through which energy from loved ones who have passed over, guides, angels and other be-ings is able to pass through. The simple version is that a medium is someone who 'talks to dead people'. However, as a 'channel', a medium is anyone open to and working with higher frequency be-ings in the Spirit realms or loved ones who have passed whether it involves bringing through wisdom, knowledge, healing or information (facts and evidence) to prove that our loved ones who have passed continue to survive after they have transitioned to the other side. In a mediumship sitting, the medium is communicating with Spirits (non-physical be-ings) outside of themselves and "the sitter" while they are fully conscious using their various heightened senses to pass on the information that is being shared – similar to a conversation you might have with anyone else. In this way, mediumship is essentially a cooperative two-way conversation between the medium and the loved one in the Spirit world.

BASICS OF ENERGY

It is essential whether you are just starting to develop your skills and abilities as a medium or if you have been connecting and blending with Spirit for some time, that you have strong and solid foundations in place for working with energy. When you have an understanding of how spiritual energy works, you can easily quieten your mind, remain grounded and centered in the present moment, let go of fears, doubts, worry and judgement, ensure your physical, mental, emotional and spiritual bodies are balanced, clear and protected, you will then be in a much better position to trust and be confident with the information that Spirit is providing for you to deliver to the person you are reading for. In this book where I refer to creating solid foundations of energy, I am asking you to ensure that you have good basic energy management practices in place before you begin connecting, blending and communicating with Spirit and loved ones who have passed over as this will allow you to be a clearer and easier channel through which those in the spirit world can connect. Below you will find a summary of the basic areas of energy management that you need to have in place – for more in-depth and practical techniques, please refer to my 'Psychic Development: Basics of Working with Spirit' book for details.

AURA & ENERGY BODIES

Each of you is surrounded in all directions by an energy field, known as your Aura, extending about 1 meter that is sensitive to all that occurs around you. It is a dynamic, living energy field, full of movement, can change colours, energy patterns and vibrations within seconds and is your personal radar system that constantly monitors your surrounding environment and works to warn you of any approaching discomfort or danger. Changes occur for a variety of reasons, resulting in light fluctuations, differences in shape (fuzzy, walled, spiky, healthy), size (large, small, absent, healthy) and the appearance of various colours which can provide clear information and insight of someone's physical, emotional, mental and spiritual well-being as well as events, situations and experiences from the past, in the present and possibilities for the future. You also have energetic bodies or layers which exist at different vibrations and frequencies that are templates for growth and development, which can be affected by energy of various types. The physical body is the one that runs, works, plays and is where you experience pleasure, pain, emotions and dreams. The etheric body is responsible for helping your body to grow and repair as well as manifest while the emotional body contains your emotions and feelings, towards self and others, as well as the ability to transform and make choices. The mental body contains thoughts, intellect, ideas and beliefs with the astral body being related to how you feel in relationships, ability to communicate needs and desires as well as where you connect to the spiritual realm. Further details and more specific information about the various shapes, size and colours that can appear within the aura and the energy bodies as well as their meaning, can be found in both the books mentioned previously which are part of this series.

It is important to be aware of the aura and the various energies that you may be connecting to whether on a psychic level by tuning into the energy field surrounding 'the sitter' by projecting your aura in front of you and enveloping the person in front of you or in a mediumship sitting by projecting your aura up and backwards into the Spirit world so that you are connecting in with the energy of loved ones who have passed over or Spirit Guides. As you begin developing your mediumship you must be consciously aware of your own energy in the way of thoughts, use of words, expressions, tone of voice, emotions, beliefs, feelings, actions, movements, mannerisms, sensations in your body or even your mood. The reason for this is that once you have projected your aura back into the Spirit realm and a loved one steps into your energy field (aura), the changes and shifts they can make can be very subtle and you must be able to connect to all of the ways in which loved ones and Guides can communicate so that you can pass on the information quickly and stay in flow with the evidence and messages they are asking you to pass on.

BALANCE & THE CHAKRAS

Each and every one of you will go through times in your life where you may experience physical injuries, stress and tension, obstacles or challenges, which can drain or imbalance the energy that flows to you and through you. It is essential when doing any work with Spirit that you ensure you are connecting from a balanced place, where you are feeling positive, loving, compassionate, confident and trusting rather than being fearful, uncertain, confused, hesitant and coming from a negative perspective of lack or doubt. You must also ensure you are balanced in your masculine and feminine energy. When you are connecting with Spirit for your mediumship you will need to ensure you embrace the masculine qualities of confidence, wisdom and knowing, power and strength as well as ensure you are focused and clear with your intention for connecting to Spirit in the first place. You will also be working with your feminine qualities of intuition, openness to receiving, communication, love spontaneity as well as your ability to surrender and go with the flow. It is also essential that you balance the giving (active, purposeful, affirming, directed and flowing outward) and receiving energy (passive, accepting non-directed and inward flow) when delivering a mediumship sitting to someone else as you will be simultaneously receiving information and evidence from loved ones who have passed or Guides that need to pass on to your sitter. Finally, it is important to ensure that your chakra system, the energy centres through which spiritual/universal energy flows in to and out of your aura, are kept in balance as well. A summary of the seven (7) main centres of energy physically and spiritually associated with various parts of your bodies, often seen and/or felt as wheels of energy, continuously revolving or rotating, is provided below.

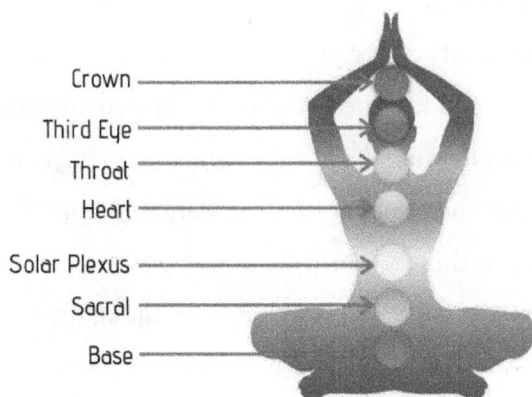

- **Crown:** Pineal gland, upper brain right eye, entry for spiritual energy/connection, enlightenment, consciousness, inspiration, higher guidance, connection, wisdom, spiritual will

- **Third Eye:** Pineal gland, hypothalamus, left eye, ears, nose, central nervous system, seeing, clairvoyance, psychic abilities, higher intuition, knowing, channelling, receiving guidance, tune into higher self, visualisation, create, purify negative and selfish attitudes

- **Throat:** Throat, lungs, jaw, vocal cords, digestive tract, thyroid, communication (thought, voice, writing), sound, expression (self, creativity, higher self/will), change, healing, transformation

- **Heart:** Heart, immune system, blood, circulation, endocrine system, emotional well-being, love, compassion, acceptance, healing, forgiveness, spirituality (bridge between physical and spiritual), emotional well-being, give and receive love (balance)

- **Solar Plexus:** Pancreas, stomach, liver, gall bladder, upper abdomen, nervous system, relationships (needs, places, things, world), connect and belong long term, contentment, trust, ego, thoughts, opinions, judgements, transform, balance, personal power, strength, creativity, passion, astral travel, connect to guides

- **Sacral:** Spleen, kidneys, bladder, reproductive capacity, sexual energy, pleasure, joy, creativity, intuition, self-worth, innocence, confidence, related to others, open, friendly, difference, separation, change, duality, movement

- **Base:** Reproductive organs, adrenals, kidneys, spinal column, survival, security, stability, safety, earth, grounded, manifestation, success, power, Kundalini, sensuality, pleasure, nourishes, perception, will-power, motivation, intent, finances

Each of your chakras, 'spin' and radiate their own unique frequency which indicates if they are open (operating normally), blocked, under-active (not open enough) or over-active (too open). When your chakras are balanced, the energy flows freely through them, you feel energetic, creative, centered, grounded, at peace and are easily able to recognise your intuition or Spirit as well as experience health, vitality and wellbeing. Below is a list of some of the ways you can ensure your chakras remain open and balanced:

- Energy Healing
- Gratitude
- Music and sound
- Yoga
- Positive uplifting people
- Sunlight
- Colour
- Herbs and Oils
- Crystals

- Affirmations
- Visualisation
- Meditation

While there are many techniques for ensuring your stay in balance, physically and spiritually, each of you will be different and you will have more success with one technique than another or may need to adjust or combine several methods until you find what works for you.

CENTERING & CONSCIOUS AWARENESS

Being centered or consciously aware, is one of the most important techniques to master before stepping into your mediumship as you have to be in the now, present to and aware of how those in the Spirit realms may work with your various senses through words, thoughts, emotions, feelings, physical sensations and much more. The information that the Spirit world brings through to you, often comes into your energy field quickly and very subtly, so you have to be open and present to what it is that they are communicating to you so you can deliver it exactly as you receive it to the person you are reading for. Essentially when centered and consciously aware you can be your authentic self, are aligned and in integrity with your values, beliefs and choices, see your experiences with compassion and from a higher perspective, are clear and able to speak your truth, confident, positive, empowered and in your strength. However, if you are scattered, not consciously aware, you can miss some of the information Spirit is sharing with you as you are in a limited, weak state of awareness, can mask or hide things, have no idea what is being shared or taking place, feel disempowered or blocked, can be too focused on the past or future, reliving old experiences, holding onto old hurt, pain and unforgiveness, repeating old patterns, over-thinking, analysing, worrying, stressing and fearful as well as pushing for things to happen when it is not the right time. So, being centered is really about making sure you gather any scattered energies into your body and shift your thoughts and emotions to a higher frequency, in other words pulling yourself together, so you can make smooth and effortless connections to those in Spirit. Below are some of the tools and techniques you can use to ensure you stay centered and consciously aware:

- Journaling
- Breath work
- Gratitude
- Food and Exercise
- Mindfulness
- Facing your Fears
- Surround yourself with positive and uplifting people
- Speaking your truth
- Releasing and let go
- Visualisation
- Meditation

Once again, try some of these techniques and see which one or combination works best to help you stay present and consciously aware in the moment.

GROUNDING

Grounding is the first technique you need to master as this is the foundation upon which everything else is built. It is something you may have practiced or used in some form or another, whether consciously or unconsciously, where you consciously connect your energy field into the physical of the Earth, that is 'grounding'. It helps you to be here in the present moment, aware of yourself physically, the sensations and energy flowing in your own body, your surroundings, what is happening in the world around you, your connection to the earth, while also striving to be more spiritual. When you are grounded you will likely experience a feeling of being connected to yourself, others, the Earth and Spirit, feel balanced in your physical and spiritual bodies, be rational and logical, conscious and aware of what is happening within and around you, be easily able to let go of any fears, doubts or insecurities so that you sit in trust and confident with who you are and your abilities, can respond to situations, events and experiences from a space of love and what feels honest for you, stand in your power and be clear mentally, emotionally, physically and spiritually. Alternatively, if you are not grounded, you may experience feelings of confusion, be in victim mode, unaware and not present, be forgetful, focused on the past/future, feeling unwell, dizzy/spaced out, clumsy, argumentative and reactive, experience headaches, flickering eyes and be sensitive to light and noise. Essentially, if you are not grounded and present with the person in front of you for a mediumship sitting, you are not going to be aware of Spirit stepping into your energy either and will not notice the information, messages and insights that you are receiving making it more difficult and a struggle. So, to ensure the information and details Spirit wants you to pass on to the sitter are brought through quickly and easily, ensure your energy is grounded by using a variety of techniques including:

- Food and Water
- Physical Exercise
- Gardening and Nature
- Animals
- Music/Singing
- Crystals
- Herbs & Oils
- Affirmations
- Visualisations
- Meditation

Take some time to experiment with the different ways for grounding your energy and use your intuition to include a technique that feels right for you.

CLEANSING

It is also important to implement a practice of 'cleansing' or cleaning the energy body of any bits of energy whether in the form of thoughts, emotions, actions, physical sensations, fears, doubts, expectations, energy cords, dirt, mud, impurities, unwanted or excess energy from not only the people and things around you that you may pick up through your day, also from those in the Spirit realms. If your aura and energy is clear you will be positive (higher vibration), focused, balanced, confident, trusting, connected, guided, flowing, energised, peaceful, rather than negative (lower vibration) where you feel unclear, confused, scattered, stressed, worried, foggy, tired/flat, stuck/blocked, lonely, lost, frustrated, controlling, fearful, doubting, over-thinking and analysing. Not only can carrying around bits of energy in your aura affect your own energy causing problems and having an effect on your daily life, it can also have a huge impact on your ability to clearly and easily connect to loved ones in Spirit and Guides and bring through information and evidence about who you are communicating with. Therefore, it is essential that you undertake a regular practice of cleansing or cleaning your energy using techniques such as:

- Plants
- Breath work
- Water
- Salt

- Clapping
- Brushing your aura
- Music
- Herbs and Oils
- Crystals
- Affirmations
- Visualisations
- Meditation

Once again, try some of these techniques and see which one or combination works best to help you stay clear and ready to connect in and work with your mediumship.

PROTECTING

As you start stepping into your mediumship, you may become more sensitive and susceptible to picking up on energy, so it is essential to protect your energy field from taking on any unnecessary thoughts, emotions, fears, doubts, patterns or problems, whether from others or those in Spirit. While you are always safe and protected, nothing can hurt you or harm you without your conscious permission, when you are energetically protected you will feel positive, balanced, centered, aware, confident, trusting, stand in your power and truth, reinforce your boundaries, neutral/detached from other's energies, grounded, clear and focused. Whereas, if you have taken on other's energies you may feel irritable, drained, not feel like yourself, negative, exhausted, be living through others, experience insomnia/poor sleep, be influenced by others, threatened, controlling/fanatical, have sudden tummy bloating, pains in neck, solar plexus or wrists or experience extreme hunger. It is essential that you protect your energy field before you give mediumship readings and can work with your Protector Guide and/or use some of the following techniques to help you with this:

- Mandalas
- Symbols
- Colours
- Herbs & Oils
- Crystals
- Angels & Guides
- Boundaries
- Living your Truth
- Mirrors
- Affirmations
- Visualisations
- Meditation

Take some time to experiment with the different ways for protecting your energy and use your intuition to include a technique that feels right for you.

BOUNDARIES

One of the most important aspects of your mediumship development is to ensure you have established strong, healthy and solid boundaries around working, connecting and communicating with those in the Spirit World. Essentially, boundaries are guidelines about what you are prepared to accept, what makes you feel comfortable, valued and loved physically, mentally, emotionally and spiritually in your relationships and connections with people both living and passed over. They are like invisible and symbolic 'fences' that, on a personal and spiritual level, allow you to:

- Gain a clearer sense of yourself and to embody 'who you are'
- Accept love, support and nurturing from others
- Reduce stress, resistance, frustration, anger and sadness and other negative impacts on your life
- Know how you want to be treated as well as how you treat others
- Successfully create and sustain meaningful and healthy relationships in all areas of your life
- Detach and protect your energy, repel negativity, drama and fear so you feel energised to move forwards in life
- Know what drains you or takes away your sense of confidence and when you may drain or take away from others
- Attract situations, experiences and people who are aligned with your intentions and values
- Honour your individual truths, ways for living and view of life and how you want it to be

27

- Draw a line, warmly and lovingly speak up and let others know if they violate any of your boundaries

Firstly, it is important that you identify what your boundaries are around working with Spirit and particularly as it relates to your mediumship in the following areas:

- **Why:** Identify why you want to do mediumship, is it just for your personal development or do you want to read for others on a professional basis. Understand what your core values and beliefs are as they indicate what is most important to you in life, what makes you feel appreciated, valued, respected and loved as well as what you see as valuable, loving and respectful in others (eg. love, support, honesty, respect, generosity). Then identify why it is important for you to connect and communicate with loved ones who have passed as well as people you may be reading for as this helps you create clear, strong and consistent boundaries around your intentions for doing mediumship.

- **When & Where:** Identifying the when and where you are comfortable connecting and communicating with those in the Spirit world as well as any people you may be reading for is essential in ensuring your physical, mental and emotional space is respected, valued and honoured. For example, are you comfortable with Spirit blending and connecting with your energy at any time throughout the day, as you are going to sleep or waking up, while you are out with family or friends while you are walking down the street, at the supermarket, bank or a café? Or are you more comfortable with establishing days, times and a space in which loved ones who have passed can connect and communicate with you so that you are able to maintain a better balance physically and spiritually? Think about how comfortable you are with approaching a complete stranger and passing on a message from a loved one in Spirit when they have not requested it as well as how comfortable or uncomfortable the other person may be and ask yourself if the location allows all involved to feel safe, supported, respected, loved and valued.

- **What:** Ask yourself questions about what it is you are comfortable and uncomfortable connecting to, seeing, hearing, feeling and communicating or discussing in a mediumship sitting? As you are connecting to people who have passed in a large variety of ways and circumstances, in mediumship sittings, it is important you understand what types of information you are comfortable with – death, infidelity, sexual details, finances, medical and mental health information. You also need to consider what your role and responsibilities are as a medium to the Spirit person, the person having the sitting and yourself as the reader particularly around privacy, decision making, free-will and permission.

- **How:** It is also important that you take the time to consider how you want to connect to those in the Spirit realms, your sense of personal space is a significant part of this boundary and determines how close you will allow Spirit and others to come to you. Also, consider whether the time you will offer sitters for mediumship connections, whether you will ask for a financial exchange for your energy, guidance and information, if you will offer sittings to family and friends or just people who you do not know any information about. It is also essential that you consider how you will deliver the information that is coming through from Spirit to your sitters and their role in making decisions and choices as a result of the information provided during a reading based on your values, beliefs, thoughts, ideas and what you feel comfortable with.

- **Who:** There are many different energies and frequencies to connect with in the Spirit world as well as in the psychical, so it is important that you establish who it is you are comfortable connecting and communicating with. While from a spiritual perspective we ALL come from and return to love, some Spirit people may have a lighter and higher energetic frequency than others who are lower and heavier vibrations such as those who may have been disrespectful, belittling and used foul language or been dismissive, ignorant and abusive in their actions when they were living as well as those who passed through suicide, drug addiction, mental health issues and/or homicides. There is no right or wrong in terms of who you are comfortable connecting with, if it makes you feel stressed, overwhelmed and fearful compared to what allows you to feel peaceful, uplifted, inspired and loving.

Once you are clear on what you are comfortable with and your spiritual boundaries, you must communicate how you want to work with Spirit and your mediumship to your Gatekeeper Guide, as their role is to ensure your boundaries are respected and maintained. In working with this Guide around your boundaries you may want to ask them to keep guard at the energetic fence or gate and to only allow people (living and passed) through who are aligned and in integrity with your boundaries, are for your highest and greatest good and are loving, kind, honest, respectful and value you, what you do and who you are. If at any time a person (living or passed) makes you feel uncomfortable, is not aligned with your values or oversteps your boundaries you can ask your Gatekeeper Guide to let you know by repelling them and keeping them behind what you might think of as an energetic fence or wall. If a Spirit person blends with your energy at an inappropriate time/place or makes you feel uncomfortable through symptoms such as sudden headaches, dizziness, clenching your jaw, heart racing, blood pumping in your ears, chills, cold-like symptoms, suddenly and inexplicably feeling overwhelmed, sad, depressed, nervous, frantic or panicked, sore neck, back or other sensations then they are violating your boundaries and you have every right to consciously tell them to stop and step out of your energy. Obviously, this is something that your Gatekeeper Guide can help you with as well, however, it is essential for you to continue strengthening your boundaries, both personally and spiritually, to communicate these with your Guide so that you are solid in your understanding of what allows you to feel comfortable and uncomfortable both in your mediumship and in your everyday life.

CONNECTING

When it comes to working with your mediumship, you must first have a strong understanding and awareness of how your intuition works, through your inner voice, deep sense of knowing or 'gut feeling', hunches or pulls that move you in a particular direction as well as being able to rely on and trust the information you are receiving. It is also essential that you understand how you can connect to and access those in the Spirit realms and receive more detailed, specific and clear information, guidance and evidence which is usually delivered through your heightened physical senses, known as the 'Clairs', through sight, sound, feel/touch, knowing, smell and/or taste. The first step in connecting to Spirit so you can develop your mediumship is by ensuring that your head and heart are working in unison to help you receive clear information and evidence from loved ones who have passed over or Guides. The head often helps you in your learning, growth and development through thoughts, words, knowledge, wisdom and even judgements that help you to recognise, think, plan, analyse, visualise, remember and understand whereas the heart helps through exploring and experiencing the full range of emotions and is the meeting point or bridge between you and those in the Spirit realms. When it comes to connecting with Spirit, it is essential that you understand that information and guidance that comes through your head compared to your heart will look, sound and feel very different with the 'head-space' often referred to as the ego (fearful self) and the 'heart-space' as the intuition (higher self). Information from your heart normally comes in response to questions, a request and is quick, consistent, repetitive, feels high vibrational, loving, light, joyful, secure, forward moving, motivating, encouraging and positive. Whereas information from the head (ego) is slow, inconsistent, disorganised, confusing, scattered, feels heavy, low, stressful, doubtful, fearful, hard, uneasy, stuck, discouraging and leave you feeling insecure and negative. Strong emotions (overwhelm) can also cloud the effectiveness of you connecting to Spirit and recognising when you receive information as it can feel muffled, clouded, distant, confused or completely blocked, so it is important for you to ensure that your head and heart are connected and working in balance with one another to receive communication from those in Spirit clearly and easily. Before you start any connection with those in Spirit through a mediumship sitting, you must ensure that you are open, flexible and in your heart-space, which you can do using a variety of techniques for tuning in and connecting including:

- Breathing
- Listening
- Ask Questions
- Tune into Feel
- Trust hunches
- Walk or Exercise
- Journalling
- Mindfulness
- Visualisation
- Meditation

It is important that you try some of these techniques and see which one or combination works best to help you connect to those in Spirit more clearly and easily, so you can work with your mediumship.

DAILY ENERGY CARE PRACTICE

Now that you have an understanding of the foundations and basic principles of energy, fundamental skills and techniques for working with your intuition and spiritual awareness, so you can tune in and communicate with Spirit more easily, it is really useful to pull all of this information together into what I call a "daily energy care practice". Like you take a shower in your everyday life, caring for your energy by having a regular routine and practice which includes techniques that feel right for you for grounding, cleansing, protecting and connecting which you can implement each day will create an incredibly strong, solid and loving foundation upon which you can begin working with your mediumship. An example of a daily energy care practice has been included below to help you understand what you might include in your own:

1 Grounding

Healthy food
Walk
Meditation (roots into the Earth)
Gratitude

2 Cleansing

Shower
Smudge
Release & Let Go
Essential Oil

4 Connecting

Intention
Spirit Guide
(Main/Gatekeeper)
Meditation (Head and Heart)

3 Protecting

Visualisation (bubble, mirror ball)
Crystal
Spirit Guide (Protector)
Affirmation

Take a few minutes to write down the techniques you will use in your daily energy care practice to support you in ensuring you have solid foundations before you start connecting in and working with your mediumship.

CHAPTER 2. MAKE THIS CHAPTER PURPOSE OF MEDIUMSHIP, RESPONSIBILITY & ETHICS

It is important that you question and understand your own values around mediumship, as the 'why' you are doing it is essential as if your purpose for mediumship is not right, Spirit retreats and you will end up doing more psychic work. The purpose for all mediumship is to prove survival of the soul beyond reasonable doubt and to represent those in the Spirit world with love, honour and respect. It is about bringing forward the evidence to prove who the 'Spirit communicator' is (beyond reasonable doubt) and that life continues after we leave this physical world. The process of conducting a mediumship connection often brings comfort, support, clarity and emotional healing for the 'sitter'. It is also essential that you ask yourself the question, 'why do I want to be a medium?' Again, the purest answer to this is not about helping people or being of service, it is about doing this work because it is what your soul needs to express. When you are doing this work with Spirit, you are also being called to strive to reach for something higher, reach for Spirit within as well as the Divine, to go within and heal, transform and grow, to rise above and move to something higher, a higher perspective. Any strengths and weaknesses in your personal life will be the same in your mediumship as your physical, mental and emotional states have an impact on your ability to do this work and be a pure channel for Spirit. For example, if you are experiencing challenges or problems in your relationships, financially or at home your energy is being pulled in that direction as an opportunity for you to create changes in these areas and then you can come back into your center and be more focused on your mediumship. In doing this work as a medium, you must also work on yourself, reflect truthfully and honestly on any limiting beliefs, patterns, fears or emotions that may be holding you back, take them as opportunities to improve and be willing to take the action steps necessary to become a better version of you and a better medium in the process.

Take a few minutes to write down your 'why' around mediumship, what is your purpose, what you value most and what draws you to wanting to connect and blend with Spirit.

Remember to trust and promote the truth of those in the Spirit world accurately, honestly and with dignity.

INTENTIONS

In undertaking any kind of work with Spirit it is essential that you set clear, direct and purposeful intentions, which are for the highest good of all, around how you wish to work with Spirit, your guides as well as your sitters. These intentions are more powerful than your hopes, wishes and wants as they set the Universal laws into motion by sending a message out asking to make them happen and asking Spirit to fully support you in honouring your intentions. Once you set your intentions, your only job is to gather your energies, keep your thoughts, words, emotions and actions aligned, in integrity with them and honour yourself, Spirit and your sitters in the process. In setting your intentions, you want to consider how it is that you intend to work with Spirit, the type of information or guidance you want to bring through, how you want to bring it through as well as how it is that you intend for your sitters to feel when they receive the reading from you as this will ensure only the highest and best information comes through.

It is also important to think about where you want to go in your personal and spiritual development, knowing precisely what you want to achieve in developing and working with your mediumship, by setting some specific, achievable goals to help you know where to concentrate your efforts and quickly spot distractions and help you to be able to measure your achievements against. Take some time to write down an intention statement which outlines how you want to work with Spirit, the type of information or guidance you want to bring through, how you want to bring it through as well as how it is that you intend for your sitters to feel when they receive the reading from you.

ROLES & RESPONSIBILITIES

When you are stepping into doing Mediumship readings, it is important to be aware of your roles and responsibilities to both the sitter and to those you are connecting to in the Spirit world. Essentially, your role as a medium is to be a clear channel of communication between the physical and Spirit world to bring through evidence (facts) to reconnect people with their loved ones who have passed as well as clarity, insight and guidance about situations they may be going through in their everyday life. As medium's who in the future or may be currently working with Spirit, you each have responsibilities when using your gift and abilities. Below are some of what I feel are the important responsibilities when connecting and working with Spirit:

- **Solid Foundations:** It is your responsibility to maintain a regular energy care practice, to quieten your thoughts/mind, step out of the way, let go of your ego so you are in the flow with Spirit and can be a clear channel for their information in ways that are loving, respectful and that value all involved

- **Sittings and Connections:** It is your responsibility to create a safe and sacred space for your sitter to feel relaxed, at ease and clear about the process you will work with and as well as what they can expect from the sitting. You are responsible for the connections you are making to those in Spirit and must be mindful of

39

what you are saying and doing at all times, making sure you bring through accurate and truthful evidence in ways that are uplifting, inspiriting, positive and empowering. It is also your responsibility to embrace each sitting with objectivity and enthusiasm, knowing Spirit is with you, to be open to the information you are receiving without judgement and to deliver this exactly as you receive it to your sitter with empathy and compassion

- **Respect and Gratitude:** You have been given a precious gift, the ability to connect and communicate with those in the Spirit realms, which is to be treated with respect and gratitude at all times. Use your mediumship abilities in a manner that shows a loving respect for all and brings comfort, empathy, support and emotional healing for those in Spirit and your sitters – it is not a party trick.

- **Honesty and Integrity:** It is your responsibility to represent the spirit world, accurately, truthfully and with dignity, to the best of your ability. It is your responsibility to be accurate and true to those in Spirit who trust you to promote and deliver their truth as they wish for it to be delivered. It is your responsibility to always work in integrity with your own values and those of Spirit and not in ways that could harm sitters or others. Remember, you can never guarantee a connection or results, so if there is NO connection - NO time = NO payment.

- **Trust:** It is your responsibility to trust what those in Spirit are giving you in the way of evidence and information and to express what you receive, without judgement or the need to persuade, convince or be right.

- **Humility:** It is your responsibility to step out of the way (leave your ego behind) and only give sittings where you have a person's prior consent (not a party trick, side-show act or for impressing people) - leave your ego at the door.

- **Evidence:** It is your responsibility to provide convincing evidence (facts) that the Spirit you are connecting and communicating with is who they say they are before passing on any messages to your sitter.

- **Honour your Individuality:** Your spiritual gifts are individual and special to you – don't compare yourself to others as you all work differently for a purpose and those in Spirit will connect with who they resonate with energetically and who can best deliver their message of love.

- **Learning and Development:** You are responsible for persistently, patiently and confidently providing the conditions conducive to being a clear channel through which your mediumship can flow. It is your responsibility to commit to learning and growing personally, lifting your vibration, meditating, work on yourself as well as to actively connecting, blending, practicing and developing your spiritual abilities on a regular basis.

You are also responsible for ensuring you are aware and present to your own energy, in the right mental and emotional state as well as connected to your heart-space, the meeting point or bridge between you and those in the Spirit realms, so that you are in the vibration of love and easily able to blend with Spirit and passing on guidance to your sitter. If you are feeling tired, stressed, uncomfortable, experiencing your own grief or the effects of alcohol or drugs of any kind, it is essential that you respect and honour yourself, your sitter and those in Spirit by not conducting the reading or postponing to a time where you are more fully in your energy and in a higher vibrational space. You may also want to consider some of the following issues that present themselves when you step into doing mediumship (or even psychic) readings for others and how you personally want to deal with them depending on your values:

- **How often will you read for a sitter?** In reading for thousands of sitters throughout the years, I have found that 3 months is a good time frame between sitters as this gives the individual an opportunity to take any actions suggested in the previous reading to bring about change and ensures they do not become dependent on you as the reader for the situations and circumstances in their lives.

- **Will you conduct sittings with couples or groups?** It is important that you consider whether you are ready to do sittings for more than one person at the same time as not only are you connecting to multiple energies physically, you will also have a variety of people in the Spirit world wanting to step forward and connect and you will need to be able to split the energy and place them with the correct sitter in order to pass on the information, evidence and guidance. You may also be asked to bring through information, evidence and guidance that is sensitive in nature and you need to be compassionate, confident and aware of the impact this may have after the couple or others leave the sitting. It is a good idea if you are starting out to get comfortable and confident with the one-on-one sittings before you step into sittings with couples or groups.

- **Will you deliver bad news?** This is an interesting one for a number of reasons. Firstly, I believe that no one can predict the future, it is never set in stone, so each person has the free-will choice to change situations and experiences that may be possibilities for tomorrow. Secondly, I do not believe that those in the Spirit realms would ever deliver "bad" news, as the information that comes from your loved ones, Guides and other higher vibrational beings "always" comes from love. Finally, yes I do believe that Spirit can give you the "heads up" on situations that may not be for your highest and best good or that you need to be aware of or take actions to prevent. Personally, I have an agreement with my Spirit Team that I will never, tell a sitter if a loved one is going to pass, mainly because I do not want that responsibility, it can have a significant impact on the sitters physical, emotional and mental well-being and mostly what if I am wrong??

- **How will you address or manage sitter's expectations?** When someone comes to you for a mediumship connection, they will often have expectations that you will be able to communicate with their loved one who has passed or to a particular loved one. Unfortunately, this can create pressure for you as the reader to meet their expectations and deliver the exact loved one they want to connect to, however, it is important your sitter knows that there is never any guarantee of a connection or that a particular person will come through. I would suggest that you address any of these expectations with your sitter at the beginning of the reading, letting them know that you have no control over who comes through or if anyone at all will come through, it will always be what they need – trust that Spirit knows what and who your sitter needs to hear from. It is also important to remind your sitter before you begin a connection that it is their personal responsibility to take the information that is brought through for them, take what fits and feels right and let go of the rest, and to take any actions that are required to change the circumstances they may be experiencing in their lives.

- **What will you do if a sitter is blocking, closed or simply there to test you?** I know it is difficult to understand why a person may ask for a mediumship sitting and then not be open to hearing what it is that is coming through from Spirit for them, whether it be emotionally, mentally or spiritually. This is neither a good or a bad thing, it is just an awareness of where the sitter is at and gives you an opportunity to talk to them a little more, set them at ease with the process, bring through some psychic insights and guidance first before stepping into a mediumship connection. It is important to be open and honest with your sitter if you are finding the sitting difficult or you are having trouble connecting, don't give up, take a few minutes to check in with Spirit and make sure you have sent your ego/fears aside, if you have and you are not getting anything say so. If you are bringing through evidence that you are confident is correct and you are receiving all no's or the sitter is unable to place the information, you may need to leave it with them until later (when it may fall in place) or know when to stop the reading if your intuition is telling you they are simply wanting to test you and be difficult as this is showing yourself, Spirit and the sitter respect. Remember, not to be tough on yourself in these situations, we all experience them and Spirit sometimes bring them your way to help you learn and grow through it and to have confidence in your connection to them.

- **How will you deal with guidance and insight around medical, legal or financial advice?** It is particularly important to remember that you are delivering spiritual guidance and information, you are NOT an expert or qualified to give medical, legal or financial advice to your sitters. You can let them know what you feel about their situation, experience or circumstances and what might be the best possible actions to take, however, you need to be aware of opening yourself up to legal action if a person follows your advice which results in detrimental consequences. For this reason, I suggest that if you have people asking for guidance around medical, legal or financial issues that you use the phrases "I am not a doctor", "I am not a lawyer" or "I am not a financial advisor" before you provide any insight around their situation – repeat it as many times as you feel drawn to so that the sitter is left knowing this and then recommend that they seek appropriate professional advice from a relevantly qualified professional.

It is essential that you do some research and to reflect on what you believe your role and responsibilities are doing mediumship sittings and connecting with loved ones who have passed as well as those who come to you for sittings. Take some time now to write down, what you feel your role as a Medium is as well as a list of the responsibilities you feel you have to yourself, Spirit and your sitters.

Learning and developing your mediumship can be fun, while also being respectful, honouring and valuing those you are communicating with in Spirit and in the sitting. It is up to you to put your fears, worries about getting the information wrong, doubts about your own abilities or the information as well as judgements or strong opinions aside as these can make the process more difficult. The more you practice the easier it will be to trust Spirit so that you can establish a strong connection, like all relationships, which will take confidence, practice and patience on your part.

ETHICS

While each of you will have different views on what is considered ethical and what is not, it is extremely important that you consider the following standards of behaviour against which you may want to work to ensure you are able to maintain high standards of integrity, respect and value:

- **Laws** of the county or state you are practicing within and whether sittings are for entertainment purposes only, complementary therapies and if you are permitted to provide sessions to children

- **Confidentiality and privacy** of clients and colleagues and whether written approval is required from the sitter in order to give out details, how to deal with life-threatening situations, slander, misrepresentation, comparisons and judgements

- **Interpretations** and suggestions about future and whether you do or do not predict the future

- **Responsibility** for choices and actions is at sitter's discretion as well as whether they are open and willing to listen to the guidance, take actions, implement decisions and choices and how frequently they have sittings

- **Questions** can be refused if you consider them to be unsuitable or inappropriate whether they are around when and if someone will pass, if infidelity is taking place in a relationship, illnesses/medical conditions, legal outcomes, breaching other individuals free will, sexuality or any other topic and you can terminate the sitting at any time - no time, energy or information provided = no payment

- **Honesty and respect** to pass on information in compassionate and non-judgmental ways to the best of your ability while being sensitivity, up-holding free-will, keeping an open heart and mind, being fully present, attentive and accepting - race, gender, sexual orientation, religion etc

- **Development of knowledge, skills and experience** is undertaken consistently whether through formal study, reading information, undertaking private training or through experience in conducting sittings
- **Operate within scope of your abilities** and area of specialisation, referring or recommending other practitioners with relevant qualifications/expertise where necessary, whether mental health practitioners, medical specialists, legal professionals or financial advisors or services with any compensation for referrals clearly outlined
- **Guarantees, promises and misrepresentations** of your abilities, services or results will not be made to promote, advertise or increase the number of sittings and sales

Take some time to do a little bit of research and reading about what other mediums have listed on their websites around their ethical responsibility and then write down your own personal ethics statement together with how it is that you want to work with Spirit.

The profound impact that delivering a mediumship connection can have for your sitter to healing from their loss, transforming and changing their lives and empowering themselves to move forward is not to be taken lightly. For me, as a medium I believe that if I can make a difference to just one person through a sitting and a connection to their passed loved one, then it is absolutely worth it - I have fulfilled my purpose. As you begin your mediumship journey or step further into your development never stop reaching for your highest potential and to find the Spirit, Universe, Source or God in not only your mediumship but also into your everyday life.

CHAPTER 3. PERSPECTIVES OF DEATH & GRIEF

At some point in life, each of you will face the loss of someone or something very dear to you and with a great loss you often experience intense emotions such as sadness, anger, frustration, guilt and much more, which are a common part of the grieving process. There are many perspectives about death and dying as well as experts who have developed 'theories' about how grief works and the stages that most people go through when they experience such a significant loss or change. Grief is a natural reaction to loss or major life changes and from a spiritual perspective a journey of learning, growth and awakening for the loved one who has passed over to Spirit as well as for those who remain in the physical world that must be embraced, appreciated and experienced rather than avoided.

PERCEPTIONS OF DEATH & GRIEF

The reality is that the death of a loved one, is something that each and every one of you will have to face throughout your journey in this physical world, whether you experience the passing of a spouse, parents, aunts/uncles, nieces/nephews, friends, siblings, pets or a child as a result of natural causes, illnesses, accidents, overdoses, war, murder or suicide, death is something that many people are ill-prepared to face. One of the reasons, that people are not prepared for the experience of death is that we are often taught, whether from a religious and/or cultural perspective, that death is something to be feared, a taboo topic, something that is uncomfortable to talk about and that you simply do not discuss. People are also often taught different beliefs and traditions about death and dying depending on many factors including religious and cultural background, with many believing there is nothing beyond this physical world, that there is no afterlife, that when you die your body simply goes into the Earth, it decomposes, and you are gone forever. However, when you look at the various religious beliefs and traditions about death whether Christian, Islamic, Hindu, Buddhist or the more Spiritual, they all believe in the afterlife in some form or another. Firstly, from a mainstream Christian perspective death is seen as a transition to some kind of heaven or hell where the person is either welcomed into the presence of God, rewarded for good deeds, freed from suffering and sin or hell where they are judged for sins in the physical world and not following the religious rules. After their passing, people of Christian faith are often buried or cremated with a funeral and memorial service, providing grieving friends, family and loved ones with a space to acknowledge who and what they have lost as well as to send them off on their transition to another kind of life. From the Islamic perspective, this present life is seen as simply a preparation for the next life, a transition, a stepping stone with death being a journey through a different dimension of existence and movement from one world to another. When a loved one of Muslim faith passes over, their body is washed, covered in clean white cloth as soon as possible after their death in preparation for burial where they are laid on their right-side facing Makkah. In Hindu tradition, there is a strong belief in the soul being reborn and reincarnated, so death is simply seen as a natural process the soul moves through as they travel to another world and then return again to continue their journey. According to Hindu tradition the body is made up of five (5) elements (fire, earth, water, air and ether) so when a loved one passes, they are cremated and are returned to each of the elements. Buddhists believe that death is inevitable and seen as an awakening process for the soul to take a break from the material world before reincarnating and being reborn into a new life back in the physical world. When a person of Buddhist faith is close to death, family and monks are called together so they can begin reciting scriptures and mantras that are intended to help their loved one to achieve a peaceful state of mind before they die.

Some perspectives of death and dying can leave people with a fear of death, which is essentially a fear of being judged and punished, as well as feelings of abandonment, permanent loss, bereavement and grief. However, the way you perceive death is a choice. You can choose to think of it as something that is final and permanent, or you can see it from a different perspective where the soul continues on an energetic journey, like a birth into a new life or into another world, where life continues in a different form and where the soul continues to learn and grow in new ways. From this spiritual perspective, death is simply seen as a rebirth, an experience that gives purpose to life, that provides limitless opportunities for expansion, connection and creation and where your relationship with loved ones continues, because we are never truly separated from those who have crossed over, it simply transforms and changes into another form.

SACRED TRANSITION TO SPIRIT

While you know that death is a part of life that each of you will experience in different ways, in order to reduce the fear often associated with dying, it is important to have an understanding of the process that a person goes through when they leave this physical world and move into the afterlife. From having worked with Spirit and connected to loved ones who have passed over for many years, it is my understanding that there is a sacred process that each soul goes through when they make the transition from one form (physical) into another (spiritual) and from one way of being into another. No matter what your religion, cultural background or belief system, this sacred transition is recognised and acknowledged by many throughout the world as an intimate journey that is to be honoured and celebrated in a variety of ways. Whether you are called to care for a loved one who is preparing for their transition into the afterlife at home, surrounded by their family or you help plan and organise their funeral service or you help get them ready for viewing before they are laid to rest either in the earth or through cremation, you are essentially helping to gently release them from their physical vessel and honouring the soul is it takes it's journey to Spirit – whether you believe in the soul's existence or not. If you can help and support them through their transition by simply holding a space of compassion, love and acceptance of whatever it is that they are experiencing, you will not only make this transition smoother and easier for your loved one, but also easier for you and your family to begin moving through the grieving process and learn, grow and transform in amazing, powerful and unexpected ways.

THEORETICAL UNDERSTANDING OF GRIEF

American psychiatrist Elisabeth Kubler-Ross suggests that to understand and cope with grief, you can split it into five stages that are often worked through, not always fitting into a neat little box or progressing from one stage to the next, in reality, there is much looping back, stages can hit at the same time or occur out of order and each person experiences it in different ways. It is important to understand that grief is a journey that people go through and make sense of in their own ways, so they can cope with the significant sense of loss and all the emotions that surface as a result. In conducting mediumship readings, you are reconnecting people with their loved ones who have passed, so it is essential you have a solid knowledge and understanding of the stages of grief as well as a general guide as to what your sitters may be moving through and how you can support them in the process.

STAGE 1: DENIAL

In this stage people often experience a sense of shock, numbness, disbelief and denial as they react to learning of the loss of a loved one. This denial and shock provides a sense of emotional protection and allows the person to cope with the overwhelming pain, loss and suffering that is the nature and reality of grief. This stage helps to not have to feel or cope with everything all at once and may last for weeks or even months for some people.

STAGE 2: PAIN & ANGER

As the shock wears off, it is often replaced with unbelievable pain, feeling like their loved one was "taken" unfairly and results in feeling completely disconnected and out of control, guilt and remorse may come to the surface over things they did or did not do with their loved one and life may feel chaotic and scary. During this stage, the release of bottled up emotions takes place, frustration gives way to anger and blame whether towards self, family, friends, the loved one who passed, or even Spirit/God, or the Universe, and the person may lash out and lay unwarranted blame on someone else. For example, anger at this stage can be focused on themselves for not taking actions that may have prevented their loved ones passing, a driver who caused the accident that resulted in the death of a loved one, at the deceased who's life was cut short due to carelessness or addiction, a spouse who drove the loved one to suicide through infidelity, or a murderer who took their loved one from them or medical practitioners they feel could have done more or arrived sooner.

Anger helps some people in this stage to feel less victimized, more in control, to honour their passed loved one and also acts as a protective barrier from the uncomfortable sadness, guilt and depression that would come by accepting what has happened. Although excruciating and almost unbearable, it is important that the person experiences the pain fully, and that they do not hide it, avoid it or escape from it with alcohol or drugs. It is important that they be aware and present to this so they are able to fully express the range of emotions that will come to the surface and to control their reactions, otherwise permanent damage to their relationships may result.

STAGE 3: BARGAINING

During this stage, people often start to question 'Why them?', attempt to negotiate pain away and try to bargain in vain with the powers that be (God, Spirit, Universe etc), family or friends for a way out of their grief and despair. It is at this time that people tend to focus on what they or others could have done differently, may want to go back in time and change things, think about all the things that could have been, how wonderful life would have been and want to negotiate in order to go back to how things were before the loss of their loved one. You may hear people say things such as 'I will never do _____ again if you just bring them back' or a variety of other 'If only ____' statements.

STAGE 4: DEPRESSION

Just when the person's friends and family members may think they should be getting on with their life, people often experience a long period of sad reflection and depression which is likely to overtake them. This brings a sense of emptiness, not feeling like they can continue, they may isolate themselves on purpose, reflect on things they did with their passed loved one, focus on memories of the past and where they finally realise the true magnitude of their loss. This sense of sadness and depression is a normal stage of grief, so it is important to allow them to experience it, do not attempt to 'talk them out of it' or try to encourage them to move on or let go at this stage as it is not helpful to their grieving. It is important to also be aware that depression can become a serious issue for people at this stage. According to the University of Maryland Medical Center, grief lasting for more than two months that also interferes with their daily life may be a sign of major depression which requires professional support and assistance. Where there are any thoughts of suicide, hopelessness or worthlessness together with an inability to function at home, work or school, it is recommended that the person seek professional help immediately.

STAGE 5: ACCEPTANCE

In this stage, the person will start to adjust to life without their loved one, life becomes calmer and more organised and the physical symptoms of grief lessen with the depression beginning to lift slightly as they begin accepting and making peace with life again. As the person becomes more functional, their mind starts working again and they find themselves seeking realistic solutions to problems posed by life and start reconstructing themselves and their life without their loved one. Essentially, they learn to accept and deal with the reality of their situation and the loss of their loved one. Acceptance does not necessarily mean instant happiness, given the pain and turmoil they have experienced, they may never return to the carefree, untroubled person that existed before this tragedy, however, they will find a way forward. They will start to look forward and actually plan things for the future. Eventually, they will be able to think about their passed loved one without pain or sadness and will once again anticipate good times to come, even finding joy again in the experience of living.

In moving through the normal process of grief when someone experiences the loss of a loved one, it is important to remember that there is no set time frame or neat progression from one stage to the next. In reality, each person will experience their own grief in their own unique and personal way that fits and feels right for them, often moving back and forwards between stages, with some hitting all at the same time and others occurring out of order. Some people also do not need to experience all of these stages in order to cope and deal with their grief, often skipping stages altogether and still coming to a space of acceptance and peace with the loss of their loved one. For others, facing the loss of someone they loved and the intense emotions associated with grief never goes away. For everyone, grief is an experience which forever changes you and your life.

Take a few minutes now to write down any experiences you have had with grief and loss the stages and what impact it may have had on you physically, emotionally, mentally and spiritually.

SPIRITUAL UNDERSTANDING OF GRIEF

For some of you, grief is a path you have or will travel many times throughout your lifetime, for others you may only have one experience, however, for all of us it is a life-shattering experience that forever and profoundly changes you. When you learn of the passing of a loved one, each of you step into the journey of grief in different ways and experience different thoughts, beliefs and emotions as a result, whether it is the sensation of your heart being ripped open, feeling hurt, scared and most of all the depths of sadness and loss as your loved one moves from this life to the next. In looking at the passing of a loved one from a spiritual perspective, it is important to understand that your loved ones in Spirit as well as your Spirit Team, are there to help and support you in moving through your grief, sadness, hurt, anger and struggle, so you can move forward and fulfil your own life's purpose and enjoy your time here in the physical world. While it may be difficult to understand at first, nothing happens for no reason, it is not random, there is always a purpose, learning and opportunity for transformation and growth if you are conscious and open enough to see it and be willing to do the work required to awaken to a new way of being in the world. Grief through the passing of a loved one, forever changes you, it opens your heart and brings with it a hidden gift for each of us to acknowledging how much we love, for without love, grief cannot exist. Also, the learning around grief, is often about understanding that you are always connected and never truly separated from your loved ones who has passed over and that their death is simply an opportunity for change, an invitation for you to connect with new experiences, worlds and ways of being in the world. In other words, grief brings you a valuable opportunity for the soul to grow and awaken spiritually, to open your heart and mind, learn to communicate with them in new and profound ways, connect to the core of who you are, what defines you in the world and reveals areas within your relationships, belief systems and values that are in need of change, transformation and healing.

Take a few moments to reflect on the loss of a loved one, what purpose it may have served, what it taught you about yourself and what opportunities for transformation and growth it opened you up to in life.

SUPPORTING YOUR SITTER

Most people who contact a medium for a reading are wanting to connect to a loved one that has passed and that was very dear to them, so they have or are experiencing loss and grief and possibly the intense emotions such as sadness, anger, frustration, guilt and much more that are a common part of the process. While a mediumship connection can support people through the process of grief as their loved one often comes through with messages to help bring peace, support and love as well as to see the higher perspective and that they are still around them, it is also important for you as the Medium to develop tools and techniques you can use with anyone who comes for a sitting with you to be able to move through the stages of grief in the best way possible for them. Firstly, to do this it is important not to try to "fix" the person's pain or sadness, it is not possible, it is an important part of their learning to feel and move through the emotions they are experiencing. All you can do is hold the space for them, to be as present as possible and simply support them through the sitting. You can also give them permission to talk and express their emotions as you simply listen with your heart because many times people just need to tell their story of grief and loss as part of their grieving and healing process which allows them to feel accepted and to be held in compassion and empathy. One strategy that might be useful for your sitter when they feel ready is to, write a 'Letter from Spirit', whether once or several times, using the following steps:

1. Sit down in a quite space where they will not be disturbed
2. Take a few deep breaths to focus their energy in the present moment and on the loved one who has passed
3. Take a pen and paper and simply start writing "Dear _____" (include their passed loved one's name)
4. Write everything and anything that comes into their mind, everything they feel, see, hear or know, no matter how irrelevant it may seem – for example clear words, thoughts, symbols, images, sounds, songs etc - just keep writing, don't stop
5. Whatever they see, hear, feel or know, follow it, ask questions about it, have a conversation with it for as long as they can

6. Continue writing until they feel the energy draw back or they feel uncomfortable and are no longer able to concentrate – this might be 20 seconds, 5 minutes, 30 minutes or an hour, whatever works for them – there is no right or wrong way to do this

7. Reflect on the messages they received from their guides, angels or directly from their loved one

You may also wish to discuss what you believe happens to a soul once they pass from this world to the next and allow the client to share what their beliefs are around this given their religious, cultural and spiritual backgrounds. You can remind your sitter that instead of struggling or pushing away the pain, sadness and grief they may be feeling to allow themselves to consciously move towards it and choose to walk through it, that is where real healing happens. It is also important to let them know there in no need to "move on" from or "let go" of their loved one as the relationship never ends, it just continues in a different form and in different ways, so it is ok for them to honour their loved one who has passed by embracing their new life and way of being. Also, people will often come to see you for a sitting around significant anniversary dates, whether it is of their loved one's passing, a birthday or other special date, which can bring up the memories of their loss and grief, resulting in the re-emerging of emotions around the date of the loss or some other important date—like a birthday. In this case, you may want to suggest that your sitter create a ritual as a beautiful and very personal way to honour the memory of their loved one who has passed over. Rituals provide people with the opportunity to bring the essence of the person who has passed over into physical form, so they can see, hear, feel, touch and acknowledge the love that they had and have for them each day. By creating a special ritual, they are also able to create and strengthen the connection with their loved one in Spirit, essentially closing the gap between the physical and the spiritual, to bring a sense of peace, comfort and love into their world. While, the rituals used will be very personal and often reflect the personality of the loved one who passed, the following are some examples of common rituals that are used to honour loved ones who have passed to Spirit:

- Planting a tree
- Creating a memorial garden
- Getting a tattoo
- Wearing a locket
- Creating a treasure chest
- Forming a charity or business
- Celebrating birthdays and anniversaries

While a client's doubts, fears, insecurities and emotions about having a sitting with a medium and connecting and receive the information from their loved one in Spirit clearly and easily, it is important to let them know that it is ok to feel what they are feeling, that their loved one knows when the right time to connect to them is and that they are always around them, only a thought away, ready to reach out and communicate, they simply need their conscious permission and participation in the process.

Take a few minutes to write down other techniques and strategies you could use to support sitters who come to see you for a mediumship reading and connect with loved ones who have passed.

It is important if you are stepping into conducting mediumship sittings, that you are able to comfortably and compassionately guide and support people in understanding that life and death are something that every one of us experiences. Share with your sitter the process that people go through when they pass over, that it can be experienced without fear, that there is no judgement, they are never lost, there is no separation and they are still connected to us, they have simply moved elsewhere, to another realm, another dimension or another frequency.

CHAPTER 4. SPIRIT TEAM & RELATIONSHIP BUILDING

In the Spirit World you have a team of guides who have chosen to work with you exclusively in this lifetime, who you can think of as your Main Spirit Team, as well as other Guides you can choose to work with at various times for specific purposes throughout your journey, think of them as your Spirit Support Team. Your Main Spirit Team are assigned exclusively to you and are available to inspire, guide and teach you, to make you laugh, help you listen, support you in resolving problems and making decisions, to provide encouragement, comfort, support, nurturing and love as well as to help you follow your passion and purpose in life. Whereas, your Support Team, including Angels, Archangels, Ascended Masters, Gods, Goddesses or the Elementals (Faery, Sylphs, Gnomes etc) who often come in and out of your life at specific times, for specific purposes, when they are needed or called upon and then leave when their work is done. Connecting and working with each of your Guides is a two-way communication process, with each member of your team intimately interested in your development, so it is essential that you build a solid relationship with them that is based on trust, respect, honour and integrity and they will work with you to bring out the best in you and in your mediumship. Let's take some time now to look at who is in your Spirit Team, their specific purpose, role and jobs as well as the importance of building a relationship with them in developing your mediumship and spiritual abilities.

Main Spirit Team

Each of your Main Spirit Team, just like each of you, have a different personality, communication style, strengths and weaknesses, areas of expertise as well as a specific purpose, role to play and jobs to do in supporting you in your everyday life as well as in your mediumship and spiritual development. While they all have the role of protecting and keeping you safe, the individual jobs they take on will be different, sometimes overlap and always require your input, as you all work together to ensure that you progress spiritually and you live a life filled with happiness, joy and love. So, let's take a look at the purpose, role and job that each member of your Main Spirit Team plays in supporting you in your everyday life as well as in your mediumship and spiritual development.

Protector Guide

Your Protector Guides main role is to keep you safe while you move through your various adventures in the physical world, whether that be in normal everyday situations or where there may be potential danger. While your Protector guide is there to help you, you must also use common sense and remove yourself from situations where there is potential harm. If you are in environments or situations where you become suddenly tired, upset, angry and overwhelmed with negative energy, whether physically, mentally, emotionally or spiritually and feel vulnerable, you can call on this guide to help repel, dispel and dissolve the negative energy. You can also ask your Protector Guide to keep harmful and negative people, situations, experiences, circumstances and energies away from you, surrounding you with people, experiences and energies that help, support, encourage and uplift your energy, as this is their area of expertise. For example, you can ask them to connect you with friends, clients, colleagues as well as situations, experiences and opportunities that value, respect and appreciate your energy as well as that are loving, joyful and in your highest and greatest good. If you are vulnerable to attracting and holding onto different energies, whether positive or negative, then it is extremely important that you understand how to communicate and connect with your Protector Guide. One way you can think of your Protector Guide is like your personal security guard, police officer, fire-fighter, solider, bouncer or body-guard, and is important in supporting you to keep you in a high vibration as you develop your mediumship.

TEACHER GUIDE

You are also assigned a Teacher Guide to work with you to help you achieve your very best, support you through lessons, encourage you to improve skills and abilities, help motivate you to want to achieve more, reach your highest potential and shine as brightly as you possibly can. Your Teacher Guide will normally have an area of expertise which is linked to your life purpose as well as the skills and abilities you need to help with your personal and spiritual development. They have a wealth of knowledge, wisdom and information to share with you, can help you open up to possible solutions to problems, lead you in the right direction as well as assist with your spiritual growth and your mediumship journey, sometimes being both the strict task master and your biggest cheerleader as you learn and grow. If you have general or specific spiritual questions you wish to know the answers to or about your path or purpose, they are your best Guide to call upon as they have access to infinite possibilities and knowledge and will provide you with the answers, whether through meditation, synchronistic events, situations, other people, books or other resources. They will also love discussing and debating spiritual topics, helping you find balance in your everyday life as well as providing help with moving through difficult situations or experiences. If you are interested in creating and writing books, offering workshops or other forms of inspirational writing, your Teacher Guide is fantastic to work with as they will help you to channel Spiritual energy, wisdom and knowledge to support you. Your Teacher Guide is like the wise elder, who is there to help teach, guide and inspire you in your everyday life, ensure you are surrounded by people and situations that will enhance your spiritual journey as well as bring you information, knowledge, skills and tools you require to help in your mediumship and spiritual development.

JOY GUIDE

Your Joy Guide is often a child or young adult and is exclusively assigned to work with you and help you to see the lighter and fun side of life as well as provide reassurance and hope for the future. They are responsible for helping you to feel good about yourself, increasing your self-esteem, help you make decisions that will bring you happiness and joy, feel confident and excited as you follow your path in life. Joy Guides often step in to remind you how to have fun and play when you have become unbalanced, weighed down or too focused on meeting your everyday responsibilities and forgotten how powerful laughter and smiling is to your health and well-being. In your mediumship development, work with your Joy Guides to help keep your spiritual vibration high so you are able to easily connect with those who wish to communicate with you from Spirit. Essentially you can think of your Joy Guide like the cheeky little child that just loves to have fun, play and express themselves authentically at every opportunity they have.

ALCHEMIST/HEALER GUIDE

Your Alchemy/Healing Guide is also available to you from the day you were born to help you maintain physical health and well-being as well as bring about changes in your energy bodies as they are particularly skilled at transforming energy within your auric field whether at the spiritual, emotional and mental levels to help prevent physical ailments and conditions from manifesting and creating challenges within your life. Because your Alchemy Guide is primarily concerned with your physical well-being, you can call on them for help and support with finding and maintaining a healthy lifestyle, including food, drink and exercise programs which will feel right for you and best suit your needs. In your mediumship work you may want to tune in and ask your Alchemy/Healing Guide for help in working with your sitter, particularly if they have any dis-eases and physical ailments presenting where they may benefit from receiving healing energy to support them in coming back into balance, ease and wellness. It is essential that you remember that any information given during a sitting around health and well-being is intended to be for guidance only and you must advise your sitter that it is not to be taken as professional, medical, psychiatric or other advice and to seek appropriate professional assistance for any physical ailments or mental health issues. For those who undertake physical mediumship, your Alchemy/Healing Guide is particularly important for helping to produce physical phenomena such as ectoplasm or transfiguration of the mediums face.

Main Guide (Gatekeeper or Guardian)

Your Main (Gatekeeper/Guidance) Guide works with you throughout your life time and plays a very significant role for developing and working with Mediumship as it is their responsibility to bring through and organise the Spirit people on the other side who are ready to connect and blend with you and pass the communication onto the sitter. This Guide will help to connect you as the Medium with sitters who are wanting and open to connecting and communicating with their loved ones, who need guidance, clarity and insight and who will appreciate, respect and value their loved one's presence as well as the services you provide in terms of being reconnected with their loved ones in Spirit, being open to feeling the loved one's presence and willing to take on board the help and guidance that is offered to them throughout the sitting. Not only do they become the main Guide for bringing through messages, guidance and clarity for own and others personal, spiritual development and growth, they also work most closely with you in your mediumship, ensuring the Spirit people are there and helping to bring through clear and accurate evidence from the Spirit communicators to their loved ones in a sitting. Your Main Guide is like your best friend, they are the first point of connection for the Spirit person who steps forward wanting to communicate through you, they organise the Spirit people for you, communicate with the Spirit person and gather the initial pieces of information and evidence on your behalf until your sitter is able to provide confirmation of who the Spirit communicator is. Once you have received confirmation and the person is able to recognise who you are communicating with, your Gatekeeper Guide will step aside so that you can begin connecting and communicating directly with the Spirit person. They will continue to help, if necessary, with the information and evidence as well as ensure that unwanted Spirits are kept away, which you may or may not be aware of them doing. Given how important their role is to your mediumship, it is essential for you to spend quality time and energy establishing a solid relationship with this Guide, getting to know who they are, understanding how they communicate with you, what their energy feels like and where they will connect with your energy as this will ensure there is a strong and consistent form of communication between you both. It will also allow you to trust the information that is coming through, be direct and clear with asking for what it is you need as well as feel more confident in connecting and blending with them and others in Spirit.

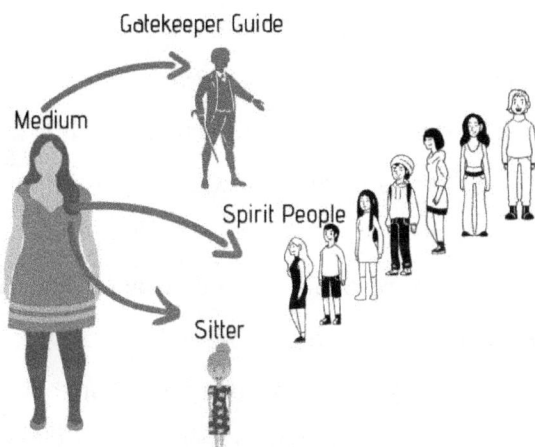

Your Main Guide may be a separate Guide or the same as one of your other Main Spirit Team who takes on this role as well as their own, whether the Joy Guide, Teacher, Healer or Protector Guide, it is important to know which one it is that you are working with. Remember, they are like your spiritual best friend, they will take care of you, help control and protect the energy field of you as the Medium as well as the sitter and those in Spirit while you are connecting and blending with them and bringing through evidence, information and guidance.

One of your Main Spirit Team will take centre stage for you to work in your mediumship, so it is important for development purposes to focus on getting to know who they are, understanding how they connect with you and their method of communication. In their communication with you they will often use the method you are strongest in to show themselves to you, however, be open to how the information is presented. You may see colours, symbols, animals, Spirit be-ings, feel energy, hear sounds etc. While it is also good to have a name to relate with your Guides, it is important not to get hung up on their name, they are happy for you to give them a name that resonates with their energy and you and to then use it regularly so that it becomes easier to access their vibration. You may also want to organise for each member of your Main Spirit Team to have specific places where they will connect with you and stand within your energy as this will help you as you are developing to be able to identify more easily who you are communicating with. For example, you may ask your Gatekeeper Guide to step in on your right-hand side and stand beside you, your Healing Guide may come in on the opposite side, your Protector Guide may step in directly in front of you, your Teacher Guide above you and your Joy guide around your knees or whatever feels right for you. By organizing your Spirit Team in this way, it helps you to be able to recognise more clearly when another Spirit links-in or blends with your energy, whether it is another guide or a person's loved one who has passed to the Spirit world.

SPIRIT SUPPORT TEAM

As well as your Main Spirit Team, you also have access to what is known as your Spiritual Support Team, who you can call on when you need them as they often connect and work with you at specific times in your life and for specific purposes then leave when their work is done.

MASTER GUIDE

Your Master Guide has a very warm, peaceful, clear, beautiful and loving energy which is of a much higher vibration than your main Spirit team. This guide is often part of what is known as the collective consciousness and can tap into and access any energy, knowledge, wisdom, insights and resources required to support you in your everyday life and your spiritual development. Your Master Guide will often bring through bigger picture guidance, messages and energy whenever needed, often during meditations and can work with other guides outside of your Spirit Team on your behalf or with other people's guides, to bring love, healing, information, resources and people to assist on your journey.

ASCENDED MASTERS

Ascended Masters are a huge group of higher vibrational be-ings who are compassionate and understanding, great inspirational and spiritual teachers who you can connect to and choose to work with when you need guidance, help and support in their area of expertise. The following are some of the Ascended Masters that you may call on and connect with together with their area of specialisation:

- **Jesus:** Helps with healing and forgiveness

- **Mother Mary:** Brings love, children, healing, fertility and mercy
- **Mary Magdalene:** Helps with independence, femininity, charity and unconditional love
- **Buddha:** Brings in balance, inner peace and spiritual understanding
- **Mohammed:** Help with communication, authority, teaching and knowledge
- **Saint Germain:** Support with spiritual purpose, transmutation, healing and protection
- **Kuan Yin:** Helps with hearing prayers, compassion, giving and receiving love and motherhood
- **Aphrodite:** Improves sexuality, marriage, romance, beauty and femininity
- **Brigit:** Brings healing, creativity and purpose to life
- **Horus:** Helps with clairvoyance, courage and strength
- **Isis:** Supports in magic work, power and self-esteem
- **Kali:** Brings protection, clears obstacles, focus and courage
- **Krishna:** Helps with joy, blessings and relationships
- **Moses:** Improves leadership abilities, helps with negotiations, clear communication and faith
- **Soloman:** Helps with magic, wisdom and manifestation
- **Thoth:** Supports with creativity, writing and teaching

ARCHANGELS & ANGELS

No matter your religious background or faith, you have no doubt heard stories of Archangels or Angels who are powerful and wonderful spiritual beings focused on helping humanity, who specialise in different types of work and are also available to protect, nurture and help you achieve your life goals. The Archangels 'oversee' all living things on Earth and the Angels in general, provide guidance and help with everyday matters, whether it is with health and well-being, love and relationships, family and children, career, business, finances, investments, study or your personal and spiritual development. You can call on a specific Archangel or Angel when you need guidance, healing, transformation, change or solutions to your everyday concerns, according to their area of expertise including:

- **Michael:** Leader of the Angels, helps with protection, courage, contacting the Divine, asserting Spiritual truth and strengthening your faith
- **Raphael:** Helps people, animals and the earth with all forms of healing as well as with knowledge and wisdom
- **Gabriel:** Communicates important messages and announcements, helps interpret dreams and visions, bring peace and transformation

- **Uriel:** Provides wisdom, dreams and visions, helps nature and to learn about God, Spirit, yourself and others
- **Raguel:** Helps bring fairness, harmony and justice
- **Ariel:** Brings courage and comfort, luck and change of fortune as well as helps reveal destinies
- **Camuel:** Provides clarity of mind and vision to help you on your path in life
- **Haniel:** The angel of joy, love, vitality and passion, helps bring new beginnings, alignment with good luck and creating positive change
- **Jeremiel:** Assists with developing clairvoyance, prophetic visions, understanding dreams, review your life and making changes to positively impact your future
- **Jophiel:** Helps with creativity, teacher of languages, provides guidance for artists, writers, musicians, architects or actors and bringing joy to the world
- **Metatron:** The Spiritual record keeper placing all that happens in the Akashic records, helps with teaching and the written word and with increasing your psychic gift

ELEMENTALS

The elementals are those from the natural world, including the Fairy (Faery or Sylphs), Gnomes (Elves, Pans), Mermaids (Undines) and Salamanders. The Gnomes, Elves and Pans are the powerful Earth elementals who work with those who show respect and kindness to Mother Earth. The Air element is represented by the beautiful winged Faery or Sylps who are drawn to work with people on projects which require mental and creative energies. The ever graceful and beautiful Mermaids or Undines are of the Water element and provide nurturing and loving care at the emotional and soul level. Finally, the Salamaders, the fire element, are often seen in the flame of a fire of candle and are fiery in nature drawing in and working with those who require more passionate energy.

RELATIONSHIP BUILDING

As connecting and working with Spirit is a two-way communication process it is essential for you build a solid relationship with each of your Main Spirit Team that is based on trust, respect, honour and integrity and they will work with you to bring out the best in you and in your mediumship. One of the most important parts of building a solid relationship with your Guides, is that you commit the time to sit and blend with each member of your team through a dedicated and consistent practice of meditation, that allows them to help raise your spiritual vibration and build your spiritual power so that you are open and ready to connect to the Spirit world. It is also important to build a solid foundation of communication, respect, trust and integrity which will require commitment, dedication, persistence and most of all patience on your part to be able to connect and work together effectively and in harmony.

COMMUNICATION

Like each of us in the physical world, your Guides will also have specific ways of communicating and connecting with you. This communication can be subtle, so it is important you spend time understanding which of your senses (also known as the 'Clair's') each of your Guides feels most confident communicating with you through as well as how they think, act and feel when they connect with you. It is also important that you spend time with each of them to establish a system of communication that works most effectively for both of you or to start learning a completely different style of communication, like learning a new language, whether through everyday life experiences and synchronicities or through your senses. In doing this you are building your relationship, so be flexible and learn to adopt your method and style of communication, way of thinking and acting depending on which Guide you are working with at the time. Remember, one of your Main Spirit Team will take centre stage for mediumship work, so it is important to focus on creating a solid relationship with this Guide, getting to know who they are, understanding how they connect and their method of communication (often your strongest sense). Like developing any relationship, it is important that you engage in open honest communication with your Spirit Team, as they do not always know everything that is going on for you in the physical world, which takes time, patience, commitment, diligence and encouragement as you build trust with each other. Schedule times to connect, ask questions and for clarity, reflect on how you are working together and make adjustments to ensure you strengthen your connection and improve how the information comes through in your mediumship sittings.

RESPECT

Whether you are a developing or working medium it is important to build your relationship with Spirit on a solid foundation of respect. Respect is not just about being polite, well-mannered and considerate it is also that deep feeling of admiration you have for someone or something because of their abilities, skills, qualities and achievements. Remember, first and foremost, you have been given a precious gift, the ability to connect and communicate with those in the Spirit realms, so treat it as well as Spirit and your sitter with respect at all times. In building this relationship of respect with your Spirit Team, you can start by scheduling a regular appointment time to sit and connect with their energy, without asking any questions or for guidance, insight or help, simply sit and allow Spirit to give you the energy you need for your development and growth, personally and spiritually – just receive their energy. To further build respect, make a separate appointment time (in advance) with Spirit when you are seeking answers, guidance or clarity about a particular issue or experience in your everyday life or with something that is happening in your mediumship, as this ensures you are present and ready to hear their answers, information and guidance. a mediumship connection – it is a two-way communication process, they can't work without you and you can't work without them – so respect the connection by turning up, being ready and honouring what Spirit is bringing through for you for your own development or asking you to pass on to your sitter.

TRUST

Trust, which according to Stephen M. R. Covey "... is based on principles of empowerment, reciprocity, and fundamental belief that most people are capable of being trusted...", is the foundation of connecting and working with those in the Spirit realms. In the physical world healthy relationships require a solid foundation of trust which takes confidence, practice and patience on your part. Connecting and blending with Spirit is no different. Trust that you do not need anything more than you already have as you will never be given anything or see, hear, feel energies on any level that you are not ready for or that is beyond your knowledge, capabilities or what you can handle. Also, to deliver an effective mediumship sitting, you must have developed a level of trust with your Spirit Team, knowing that they completely support you and being confident in the information that is coming through. It is also your responsibility, once the Spirit person blends with your energy and steps in closer to begin working with you, to build trust with them by accurately and truthfully passing on each piece of information they give you. As you begin to pass on the information you are given (without doubting or judgement), the Spirit person will begin to draw closer to you and start working with you more, bring you more details and evidence as you have demonstrated to you are capable of being trusted. This may be easy for some of you if you are easily able to quieten your thoughts, get out of your own way and trust the information that Spirit is providing you. For others, fear of getting the information wrong or doubts about your own abilities or the information you are being given can make this process more difficult. You must be willing to let go and start regularly connecting and communicating with Spirit so it becomes easier to step out of your own way and you can build a solid foundation of trust with Spirit.

INTEGRITY

Again, like any relationship in the physical world, honesty and integrity are essential to ensuring you work together effectively and in harmony. To build a solid foundation of integrity with your Spirit Team, as well as passed over loved ones, you must bring through the facts, evidence, information and messages you are being given accurately and truthfully to the best of your abilities. Remember you are a representative for the Spirit world here in the physical, so always work in integrity with your own values and those of Spirit, be accurate and true to those in Spirit who trust you to promote and deliver their truth as they wish for it to be delivered. This means bringing through information with compassion, dignity and love not in ways that could be hurtful, damaging or traumatic to the sitter or others in their life. Remember, you can never guarantee a connection or a particular result in a mediumship sitting, so you must be honest if you do not feel you have a connection to a passed loved one tell your sitter "I don't have anyone coming through at the moment" and take a moment to connect back with your heart space, raise your spiritual vibration, get into the zone and connect again, starting with a few words. If you still have nothing coming through, don't panic, don't go into your head/fear and a story about not being good enough or that you can't do it, simply trust that there is no connection for a reason and go back to your Spirit Team and seek guidance and support around what may have taken place so you are aware for next time.

ROLES & BOUNDARIES

Each of the Guides who have been chosen to work with you, like each of you, will not only have specific ways of communicating and connecting, they will also have different and particular roles, like those outlined in a Job Description, which can sometimes overlap, to support you in everyday life and your spiritual development and growth. It is important that everyone involved is clear on what role they are playing and what tasks they are responsible for, so you must take the time to connect with each of your Guides and clearly agree on and assign each individual role as well as establish your boundaries in terms of how, where, when and with who you want to work with in Spirit and in your physical world. You can do this by simply going into meditation with your Spirit Team, asking them to identify themselves and to bring through information or something that identifies which job/role they feel they fit best in working with you in your mediumship. While one of your Main Spirit Team will take centre stage, think of them as the Manager, you as the Chief Executive Officer (CEO) must understand the role that each member of the team plays and focus on creating a solid relationship with each to ensure all components are working cooperatively, in unison and in the most effective way to bring out the best in your mediumship.

My **Connecting with your Main Spirit Team Meditation** will take you on a journey to meet each member of your main Spirit Guide Team so you can get to know what their energetic vibration looks, sounds and feels like, begin communicating with them and learning about their personality, how they best connect with you as well as their strengths and weaknesses, the specific purpose they play in your life, their role in your personal and spiritual development and where any changes, transformation or healing may be required. You can also take the time through the meditation to ask each of your Guides about their area of expertise, what skills and abilities they can help and support you with, assign each within your team specific jobs and tasks that you would like them to take on as well as your personal and spiritual boundaries in order to support you in your everyday life as well as spiritual with your mediumship.

Take some time to write down details about your Protector Guide, Teacher Guide, Joy Guide, Healing Guide as well as your Main Spirit Guide (Gatekeeper) together with any messages, insights, guidance and information provided around your everyday life or your personal, professional and spiritual development and growth.

CHAPTER 5. CONNECTING & BLENDING WITH SPIRIT

By now you understand that it is extremely important to undertake good basic energy management before you begin communicating with Spirit and loved ones who have passed over. As the energy of Spirit is vibrating at a different, higher, faster rate from that in the physical world, to make connecting and communicating easier and more fluid you need to open your energy field and awareness to Spirit and undertake regular energy practices that help you to raise your spiritual vibration and meet them halfway. Once you have lifted your vibration, it is essential that you develop a practice of sitting in the power of Spirit as this allows those in the Spirit world to support you in further developing your mediumship and with your personal learning and growth – which goes hand-in-hand with your mediumship – as well as moving the logic mind out of the way to allow you to trust the information you are receiving from Spirit. Because mediumship is all about bringing through facts and evidence that proves the soul continues after we pass from this life to the next, the next step in the process involves connecting and blending with the Spirit world which is essential in ensuring you are able to receive the information you need to pass on to your sitter in a reading. Let's take a look at the various ways you can lift your vibration, build your spiritual power and the blend and connection with Spirit.

RAISING YOUR SPIRITUAL VIBRATION

When you raise your spiritual vibration, you begin to resonate at a higher frequency which increases your awareness and connection with Spirit. When you feel fearful, heavy, stuck, negative or down your spiritual vibration would be considered low, however, when you feel loving, light, free, positive and up your vibration is high. There are a variety of ways to consciously raise your spiritual vibration to a 'higher' state, bring yourself into a 'higher' state of awareness, so Spirit can meet you halfway and make connecting and communicating easier. Some examples of how you can raise your spiritual vibration include:

- Purifying your body by eating fresh fruits and vegetables, whole grains, nuts etc as well as drinking plenty of water
- Engaging in exercise whether it is running, walking, yoga, rock climbing, swimming, tennis, basketball, soccer etc. exercise is will increase your energy
- Focus on positive thoughts and emotions as fear-based thoughts and feelings such as anger, sorrow, guilt, hatred, despair, fear, jealousy and frustration lower your vibration you can work with affirmations to shift your energy and bring you into higher vibration

feelings such as love, respect, appreciation, joy, happiness, hope, strength, peace, trust and faith

- Surround yourself with uplifting, positive people, or with a beautiful, peaceful or happy environment
- Meditate and learn to quieten the mind by focusing on your breath and listening to your heart
- Practice gratitude, appreciation and compassion by remembering how blessed you are and by helping others less fortunate than you
- Journal to reflect on and explore your own personal experiences and to grow mentally, emotionally and spiritually
- Spend some time outdoors in the water or connecting with nature and Mother Earth
- Work with crystals, music, sound, art or dance
- Smile, laugh and do things that bring you joy and that you are passionate about

The techniques you use to help you raise your spiritual vibration will vary depending on what it is that is going on in your everyday life and you may find that one or more techniques are more effective than others for you. Take some time to write down, which techniques were easier for you to undertake and were more effective in helping you raise your vibration.

BUILDING SPIRITUAL POWER

Once you have undertaken a process to raise your spiritual vibration to meet and connect with those in the Spirit world, it is important to commit to sitting with Spirit on a regular basis to build your spiritual power. When talking about building spiritual power, you are essentially being asked to sit in the silence within, embrace the power of your own spirit and connect to Source, Universe, God and the oneness of all that is. The best way to do this is through a process of meditation, which not only helps to raise your spiritual vibration, it also clears your mind, let go of problems, helps you gain clarity on your path, provides answers to your questions as well as increases your awareness and connection with Spirit resulting in advancing your mediumship abilities more quickly. While many of you may have been taught different techniques for how to meditate, it is important you find a method that works best for you, whether it is sitting in complete stillness or undertaking a moving meditation practice – both work the same way. The intention for this type of meditation is to simply sit, be at One with Spirit and to build your spiritual energy for your own personal and spiritual development by clearing your mind, letting go of your earthly thoughts, feelings and actions so that you can simply sit in the power with Spirit. Whether you visualise and go to a spiritual sanctuary, special place or heart space, it is important to remember that this is a time for you to simply receive the energy from Spirit so that you can connect with them with ease and grace, it is not the time to seek answers or solutions to any problems you may be experiencing. If you have questions, want solutions or are seeking guidance in relation to particular areas of your life, make an appointment to connect with Spirit at a different time to receive this information. By simply starting to be conscious of your breath - even if it is just for a few moments—and your connection with Spirit it will help you to build your spiritual power and make a huge difference in both your everyday life and in your spiritual development. Don't skip over this process, you must make a commitment to do this at a regular time every day for at least ten (10) minutes, longer if possible, so you build discipline and consistency in your work and Spirit will turn up for you like you turn up for them. By building your spiritual power every day you are also reminding yourself of your constant connection with Spirit which will free you to receive the gifts that are being offered to you in each and every moment throughout your everyday life and in your work with Spirit. Remember, to reach your full mediumship potential you must commit to connecting and building your spiritual power and have a routine where you sit quietly, preparing to start work and accept the energy from those in the Spirit world.

My **Sitting in the Power with Spirit Meditation** is a really simple meditation which can be used on a daily basis to support you in your personal and spiritual development by allowing you to raise your vibration to meet and connect with those in the Spirit World in order to receive their energy for your own learning, growth and development.

Take some time to Sit in the Power with Spirit through meditation and then write down what day and time works best for you to do this on a consistent basis, what was the energy that Spirit asked you to be open to receiving and working with, how did you feel, what changes did you notice and what insights and learnings did you get from this process.

GETTING IN THE ZONE

When you sit with Spirit to support you in building your spiritual power you are essentially getting prepared to start your work with Spirit or in other words 'Getting into the Zone' in terms of connecting, communicating and providing evidence to your sitter. What you are doing is moving the mind out of the way, moving your awareness away from the physical world and towards Spirit so you get into the receiving mode by turning your attention within. When you do this, there will be an internal shift, a change in the energy or power, as you move into 'The Zone' – if you are struggling to know if you are in there, you are not there yet keep sitting in the power of Spirit. The shift or 'The Zone' will feel different for everyone, it may be like a daydream state, you may see energy similar to heat rising off the road or just don't feel as crisp and clear as normal. If you are thinking about anything else other than receiving the perceptions, impressions and evidence from the Spirit world, you are not in the zone and need to come back to you and focus within. Once you are in the zone, this is when you can begin connecting and communicating with those in the Spirit world.

Take some time now to become present to and aware of when you are ready to start your work with Spirit, that is what does 'The Zone' look like, feel like or sound like for you. Then write down what shifts or subtleties you noticed take place with your energy so you know when you are connecting, communicating and ready to provide evidence to your sitter.

CONNECTING AND BLENDING WITH SPIRIT

You may have been taught, shown or read about many different methods for connecting and blending with loved ones in the Spirit world, including opening all of your chakra's from the base chakra up to your crown etc etc etc. Yes you need to calm your mind, build your spiritual power so you are closer to Spirit and be open and receptive to sensing and communicating with Spirit, however, all you need to do is set an intention or invite Spirit to step in to connect with you and they will blend with your energy and start communicating and simply acknowledge that you already have a connection with Spirit. Some of you may find that you are more receptive to connecting with Spirit as you fall asleep and/or just before you wake up, while you are daydreaming or in a meditative state. This is normally the case because your mind is calm and not filled with thoughts about your every-day life which is why it is essential to continue lifting your vibration and building your energy before you start working with them. It is important though when you are ready to connect to Spirit that you consciously ask the ego, your fear or logical mind, to step to the side so you can tune into the non-physical energy of those in the Spirit world, allow their voice and essence to come through you and be able to deliver the information and evidence relevant to the person having a sitting with you in the easiest and quickest way possible.

As you shift your awareness from your physical being, step out of the way, open up and invite Spirit to 'blend' or 'link in' with your energy, you will generally feel your aura or energy field being drawn behind you, unlike with a psychic connection where you connect with the energy of a physical person in front of you. Once you establish the initial link with the Spirit person, you may sense or become aware of them stepping in closer, feel like the air on one side of you becomes denser or thicker, see them standing beside or behind your sitter or see their energy like heat rising from a road. As this happens, it is important that you keep drawing your energy or awareness back to the Spirit world and begin working with them to bring through evidence (facts) and information to confirm who it is that you are communicating with as well as their essence and eventually pass on messages to their loved ones. It is your responsibility to control the link you have with the Spirit person, to keep drawing your energy or awareness back to them, inviting them to step closer, rather than allowing the sitter to take control and pull you into a psychic connection instead of a mediumship connection. One of the easiest ways to ensure you draw your energy back to those in Spirit, is to not look directly at the person who is wanting the mediumship connection, look off to one side and into the distance which ever feels more comfortable for you and allows the Spirit person to create a stronger link with you as the medium. Once you become aware that Spirit has connected and blended with you, you are now ready to receive information from them and be the channel between those who have passed over and their loved ones who are here in the physical world.

CHAPTER 6. RECEIVING INFORMATION THROUGH THE SENSES

There are different types of information you will receive from passed over loved ones to provide in a mediumship sitting all of which will come through your heightened physical senses known as the 'Clairs'. As the Medium, you are essentially acting as the bridge for communication between the spiritual and the physical world and may hear (clairaudience), see (clairvoyance), know (claircognizance) and/or feel (clairsentience) messages from those in Spirit with the intention of healing both worlds. You never know how the information will come about (through which senses) until you open your mouth and begin to speak so you must be present, acutely aware of what drifts into your energy and open to all possibilities. Let's take a look at how you receive information through each of the senses.

RECEIVING THROUGH THE SENSES

Those in the Spirit world may bring information, facts and evidence through your sense of sight, sound, feel, knowing, smell and/or taste and use your own experiences, frames of reference, beliefs, ideas as well as symbols to help you be able to quickly and easily understand what they want to deliver to your sitter during the communication. It is essential when you are receiving information you are present, conscious and aware so you notice everything they are bringing through as the information can be subtle, easily missed and may come through in a different way than you are expecting. Let's do a quick refresher on how you might receive information through each of your heightened senses known as the 'clairs'.

CLAIRVOYANCE

Clairvoyance is commonly known as 'clear seeing' and is the ability to 'see' or 'perceive' images and visions beyond the physical world and into the spiritual realms, whether of passed over loved ones, Spirit Guides, Angels, Archangels etc. These visions can be experienced on a physical level, however, are generally flashed very quickly into the medium's mind through their spiritual eye (3rd eye), mind's eye or inner seeing so they can be described during a sitting or when giving a message. You may receive information clairvoyantly as a glimpse of Spirit people and Guides through the corner of your eye, see the colours in people's auras or sometimes see Spirit as tiny sparks of light, transparent orbs or beads, shadows or a normal figure standing in front of you or moving to one side. Many people as they first start developing, expect to be able to see Spirit as clearly as they see other people in their everyday lives, however, it is important to let go of all expectations about how this happens and to allow your 'clear seeing' to come in at the best time and in the right way for you.

In a Mediumship sitting, you as the Medium may begin receiving information and evidence from passed over loved ones through your Clairvoyance like a movie being projected and played into your mind's eye or spiritual sight or have images and visions displayed on a whiteboard or black board for you to then pass on to your sitter. For example, Spirit may write their name on the whiteboard for you or you can have the alphabet displayed and ask them to circle or highlight the first letter in their name. You can also work in this way to ask for the Spirit person's date of birth or date of passing by asking them to write the date, year and month or you can have them circle or highlight the relevant information on a calendar displayed on the screen or board. You may also see images and pictures projected of where the Spirit person lived, locations that were important and significant to them when they were in the physical world, places that your sitter and the Spirit person visited, a memory of a special time at a location with your sitter or other members of the family or people they want to include in the sitting. You could also be shown through your clairvoyance an item of jewellery that belonged to the Spirit person and may have been gifted to the sitter or another member of the family, an object that was important or significant to both the sitter and passed loved one. Those in the Spirit world may also show an image or display a symbol to show their relationship with your sitter, the type of work they did, how they passed, hobbies and other activities they did when they were still in the physical world, so it is a good idea to build your own Spiritual Library or Spiritual Dictionary of image and symbol meanings you would like Spirit to provide you with in your sittings. For example, those in the Spirit world could show you any of the following common symbols to represent a piece of information, evidence or a message that is to be passed onto your sitter:

The possibilities for the types of symbols, images and visions Spirit can bring through to provide evidence in a mediumship sitting are limited only by your imagination.

One of the best ways to develop your Clairvoyance and ability to 'see' or 'perceive' images and visions during your mediumship sittings is to improve your observation skills in the physical world by simply finding a location somewhere in public where you can sit and observe people, the environment and your surroundings. While observing what is taking place in the physical world around you, start consciously describing, out loud or on paper, what you are seeing, around you, whether you start by describing your environment, any objects or shapes around you, what colours you can see, if there is any traffic around, then start describing the people who are present, how tall they are, their build, what colour hair they have (if any), the shape of their face, their complexion, how they are dressed, if they have any scars, tattoos or interesting features. This will help those in the Spirit world to gain an understanding of how you perceive and describe what you are seeing and also build up your Spiritual Library or Dictionary they can use and place in your awareness during a sitting to make it easier for them to bring through the information and evidence and work with you. Another good way to strengthen and develop your spiritual sight and ability to see is to practice doing remote viewing which allows you to gather information about various things including people, places, objects, environments or events, that are not accessible to the normal senses because of distance, time or shielding. Remote viewing has been used throughout history by the CIA and the US military as a technique for gathering information and insights including details about lost objects, where people are located, what someone may be doing as well as solutions to various problems. To conduct a remote viewing session, it is important to set a clear intention and to be specific about what or who your specific target is that you are wanting to tap into and 'view' remotely and then describe or give details about. While your specific target in a session can be many things including a person, place or an environment, in the context of a mediumship sitting, your specific target would be a loved one in the Spirit world who you want to gather information about and then simply describe using statements of fact about their physical appearance, what their home, workplace or school looked like or even a favourite location or an environment where a significant event took place. This is one of the best ways to practice asking a specific loved one in the Spirit world to step forward and connect with you, refine your questioning skills as well as your ability to deliver facts and statements that require a 'yes' or 'no' only answer from your sitter. The following is a really simple process you can start using to conduct a remote viewing session:

1. Close your eyes and take a few deep breaths to relax as you get yourself into a space to connect with the Spirit world

2. Ask your conscious mind to step to one side, invite your Main Spirit Guide to step in to support you throughout the session

3. Set a direct and clear intention of who in the Spirit world you wish to connect to and what specific information it is you want to gather

4. Focus your energy on your target person in the Spirit world and allow any images, visions and colour to come into your awareness

5. Dig a little deeper by asking for more specific details like colour, shape, location, environment, etc., until you feel you have enough information

6. Open your eyes and write down everything that you saw, felt and thought during your remote viewing session

7. Deliver the information gathered to the person you are doing the session for and check your accuracy

8. Once you have finished, disconnect from the Spirit person and clear your energy

Remember, to keep an open mind and let go of expectations about the types of images, visions, symbols or colours that may come through in a remote viewing session or in a mediumship sitting, as those in the Spirit world will work with you to support you in developing this sense in ways that fit and feel right for you. It is also important that you have patience with yourself as you are learning and remember that the more you observe and acknowledge what you are seeing in the physical world the more you will develop your skills as you move forward.

CLAIRAUDIENCE

Clairaudience is essentially 'clear hearing', which means you are able to hear sounds, noises or words, either on a physical level or as a voice in your head which are different from what your own mind chatter sounds like, from those in the Spirit world whether that is your own Spirit Guide or someone's loved one who has passed over. Through this sense you may hear a sound or words with your physical ears that other people can often also hear that come to you spontaneously and quickly or as internal words or sounds that no one else but you can hear and float into your awareness like thoughts but have a different tone and pitch than your own voice. There are a variety of ways that you can experience your Clairaudience, whether voices talking, music playing or a high-pitched ringing sound, sudden ideas and inspiration flow into your awareness, a loud noise which gets your attention, hear someone call your name or say something to you only to find they didn't say anything at all or randomly thinking about a loved one in Spirit or other people while driving, cleaning the house, doing the dishes or other mundane tasks. In a mediumship sitting the information and evidence you hear from those in Spirit through Clairaudience may sound quiet, loud, friendly, direct, firm, bossy and pushy depending on their personality, it will always be loving, nurturing, supportive and uplifting. For example, you may have a passed loved one step forward and tell you their name, the name of the sitter or another family member, dates that were relevant to them or the sitter, words or sayings, sentences or entire conversations, music or songs that have a special meaning, traffic noise or other everyday sounds. It is important to keep an open mind and let go of expectations about how the information is brought through from those in Spirit for you through your hearing whether it is sounds, noises or words, sentences, sayings, music or other pieces of evidence and trust that it will come in at the right time and in the right way for you.

To develop and improve your Clairaudience, it is important to learn to observe silence by focusing inwardly whether through conscious breathing or meditation and to spend time in your own company listening, without speaking, dialogue or holding any type of conversation, becoming aware of your own thoughts and words as this will help you discern what is your own voice compared to Spirit's voice. You can also work on your clairaudience abilities by practicing active listen and really tuning in and focusing in on all those little sounds in your everyday life that you normally don't pay attention to and ask yourself 'What do I hear?' This will help you to be able to more easily hear and recognise information and evidence that a passed over loved one may want you to deliver to your sitter whether it is their name, age, their relationship with your sitter, how they passed over, their personality, sayings, songs, music and or memories from when they were in the physical world. Receiving information through this sense can be confusing at first as you try to distinguish whether what you are hearing is your own thoughts or a message coming through from Spirit, the more you work on developing it the easier it will become to distinguish the voice of Spirit from your own.

Note: There are some medical conditions such as schizophrenia and multiple personality disorder where people do hear repetitive, uncontrollable and negative voices. In these cases, please seek advice from an appropriate medical professional as soon as possible.

CLAIRSENTIENCE

Clairsentience, 'clear feeling' or 'clear sensing', is the ability to feel things and to sense intuitive information and evidence whether in relation to environments, places, people, situations, events as well as Spirit Guides and loved ones who have passed over. Those who are highly sensitive clairsentients, known as empath's, are easily able to put themselves in the other person's shoes, see through lies and deception, tune-in and actually feel other people's emotions as if they were their own, sense other people's thoughts and beliefs as well as pick-up and feel others physical pains and illnesses in their own body. If you are clairsentient, you may be able to easily understand the thoughts, beliefs emotions of your partner, family, friends, colleagues or clients, even if they are at a distance, and sense if they are feeling anxious, stressed, alone, sad, fearful, doubtful, unhappy or depressed or if they are happy, joyful, enthusiastic or peaceful even when the other person may not be outwardly displaying these emotions. You may also experience information coming through this sense in a number of different ways whether as a 'gut feeling', warmth or a butterfly sensation in the stomach area, shivers go through your body or the hairs on your arms or the back of your neck stand on end unexpectedly or energy and vibrations coming into your aura to let you know to embrace or stay away from a particular person, situation or place.

Because empath's are highly sensitive people with strong clairsentience abilities essentially use their energy field as a vibrational detecting device, they must have strong energy management practices in place and learn to distinguish between what is their own thoughts, feelings or physical sensations as well as how their physical environment or certain places, situations and people make them feel so they can easily discern when the energy around you changes. This is incredibly important for your mediumship as you must be able to also recognise when someone from the Spirit world steps in to connect with you through this sense and feel when your own energy shifts as it is often changes in very subtle ways that you must be present to and be able to discern whether it is yours or a piece of information or evidence from a passed loved one.

In a mediumship sitting the Spirit person you are connecting with may give you different pieces of information and evidence using your sense of feel to indicate who they are, whether gender, relationship to your sitter, how they passed over, height, weight, body shape, personality, gestures, mannerisms or habits that were significant, their emotional state/well-being prior to passing or details about your sitter's emotional state/well-being. If a Spirit person makes you feel their presence whether as a subtle shift and change in the temperature or density of the energy on the left side of your physical body they may be letting you know that you are connecting with a female Spirit person, whereas if they step-in on the right side you may be working with a male Spirit person. You may also have those in the Spirit world step-in wanting to show you their relationship to the sitter by placing their energy on your body, almost using your physical body as a timeline to show you how they were connected. For example, you may ask those in the Spirit world to show you their relationship to your sitter by placing their energy on your body as shown below:

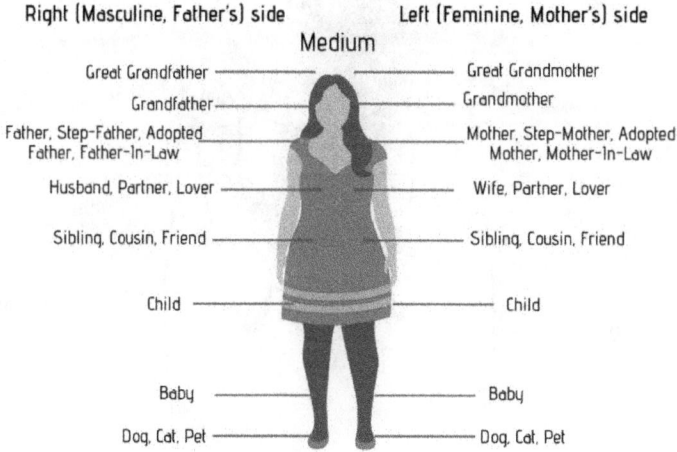

Right (Masculine, Father's) side   Left (Feminine, Mother's) side

Medium

Right side	Left side
Great Grandfather	Great Grandmother
Grandfather	Grandmother
Father, Step-Father, Adopted Father, Father-In-Law	Mother, Step-Mother, Adopted Mother, Mother-In-Law
Husband, Partner, Lover	Wife, Partner, Lover
Sibling, Cousin, Friend	Sibling, Cousin, Friend
Child	Child
Baby	Baby
Dog, Cat, Pet	Dog, Cat, Pet

If Clairsentience is one of your strongest senses, you may also receive information from those in the Spirit world about any health conditions they experienced, how they passed over or any health conditions your sitter may be experiencing through this sense by them placing energy around a particular organ or area of the body. See below for information about where the major organs are located in the human body:

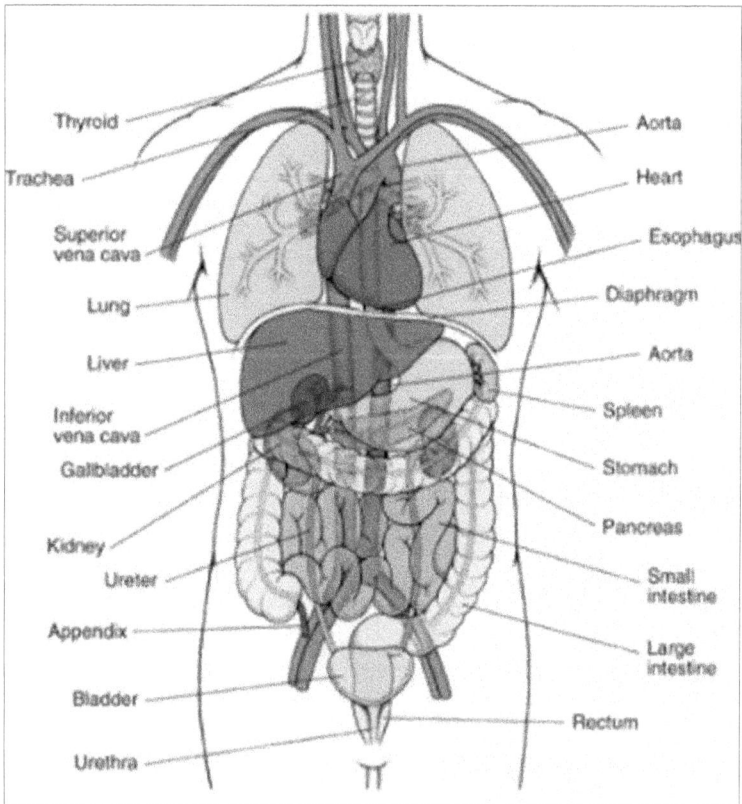

Thyroid
Trachea
Superior vena cava
Lung
Liver
Inferior vena cava
Gallbladder
Kidney
Ureter
Appendix
Bladder
Urethra

Aorta
Heart
Esophagus
Diaphragm
Aorta
Spleen
Stomach
Pancreas
Small intestine
Large intestine
Rectum

You may also find that Spirit will work with objects that they want to remind their loved one of by placing them in your hands, so you have to be present to when this happens, notice the energy, slow down and explore it in more detail by talking to Spirit and asking them to show you what it is you have in your hand. For example, in a mediumship sitting you may have an item of jewellery, a trinket, a walking stick or a variety of other items placed in your hands energetically that you need to feel into and describe in detail to your sitter.

To improve your clairsentient abilities, one of the best divination tools you can work with is psychometry, as this allows you to use your sense of touch to hold an object and pick-up on a person's thoughts, emotions, beliefs, experiences and circumstances in life. A really simple way to do this is to have someone give you a photo/picture of somebody you don't know but they know well and simply tune into their energy, whether through their eyes or by just setting an intention, then asking how they felt when the photo was taken. You may initially pick up on a feeling of lightness or heaviness, positivity or negativity, love or fear, then dig deeper by asking about the individual's personality, what they are like as a person, what they value most, whether they are trustworthy or not, how they behave and how they view the world. Once you have finished bringing through the information, ask your friend to provide you with feedback about how accurate you were in describing the person in the photo/picture. You can follow the same process using a photo/picture of somebody's passed over loved one and invite them to step forward and talk to you about who they are, how they passed, where they lived and what they enjoyed doing in life as this will help you to be able to remain focused on asking for facts and evidence to prove who they are to your sitter.

You can also improve your clairsentience abilities by observing and spending time in a busy place, like a shopping center, coffee shop, park or other public place, where you have full view of the people who are arriving and leaving. Simply choose one (1) person, to focus on and tune in noticing what it is they are feeling, are they happy, excited, tired or upset? Then feel into who they are by asking for information about their personality, if they are married or in a relationship, whether they have children and how many, the type of work they do or if they are studying etc. Allow your 'sense of feeling' to guide you, explore who they are at a deeper level, practice regularly, increase your awareness of how you receive information and guidance in this way and it will become easier to recognise and improve your ability to feel those in the Spirit world as they step forward to connect and communicate through you.

CLAIRCOGNIZANCE

Claircognizance or 'clear knowing' is the ability to clearly know information or about experiences that have happened in the past, present or will happen in the future, often without knowing how you know. You may experience your sense of 'knowing' as a thought, message, idea, insight or information that just "comes to your mind" in a flash and then goes, that you have no idea where they came from, like lightbulb or 'A-ha' moments that you are 100% certain in your body is true and something that cannot be denied. If you suddenly receive solutions to problems, know the best decision to make, experience nagging and persistent thoughts about people or situations, know when someone is being genuine and is trustworthy or if they are lying and being manipulative, have a knowing not to go somewhere or do something or are inspired to create or do something new and different, this is your Claircognizance at work. You will often receive information through this sense at random times, when you are doing tasks that are different or completely unrelated, such as working, driving, walking, cleaning or doing another task which is almost automatic. If you have an innate sense of 'knowing', you will tend to be more logical, easily understand abstract concepts, enjoy thinking things out and analysing, are a problem solver, like researching and gathering information, learning through books and written word and may have been labelled as a 'know it all' by others.

In a mediumship sitting, you will be given answers to your questions, whether it is 'who', 'what', 'where', 'why', 'how' or 'when', from the person in the Spirit world by having the information and evidence 'pop into your head' or your mind as if it were your own thought when you receive through your Claircognizance for you to pass on to the sitter as confirmation that they are still with them. For example, a loved one who has passed over and is connecting with you, may bring through information and evidence about what they did for work and you may just 'know' that they worked with their hands, know that they worked with tools in their hands that were metal and then have a thought drop into your awareness that they worked on cars and so you know that the person was a mechanic. This is often one of the most doubted of the senses to work with during a mediumship sitting as it will require you to take a leap of faith, trust what you are being given and risk getting the information wrong, especially when you are first developing and learning to discern your own thoughts from that of Spirit. As you start working with your sense of knowing more consciously and giving the information exactly as it comes in, you will know with 100% certainty in your body when it is true and accurate, building your confidence and trusting that sometimes the information will only make sense in hindsight, when you look back and after it has been delivered to your sitter.

One of the best ways to develop and improve your sense of 'knowing' is by practicing automatic writing as it allows you to connect with those in the Spirit realms and to simply bring through their thoughts, words, ideas, evidence and information through your hand without the logical mind getting in the way and you overthinking what you are receiving. To practice automatic writing, you can simply take a pen and paper to a quiet space where you won't be interrupted, hold the pen loosely in your hand, connect in with those in the Spirit world and ask someone to step forward and connect with you. Once you feel the energy shift and someone steps in to communicate with you, simply allow your hand to move when it feels right - don't try to force it. You may feel the energy running through your arms or hands, like a tingling sensation as the Spirit person begins communicating and bringing through the information or message, which may appear in a disjointed, unorganised and unusual way with incorrect spelling and completely different grammar and hand writing than your own.

CLAIRSCENT OR CLAIROLFACTION

Clairscent or Clairolfaction, is essentially 'clear smelling' which means the ability to 'smell' or 'perceive' energy, smells and scents, pleasant or unpleasant, whether physically or spiritual, that come from those in the Spirit realms. You may experience your sense of smell come in as a fragrance, perfume, flowers, food, herbs, spices, urine, dirty laundry, smoke (tobacco, timber, burning candles, fireworks etc), chemicals (alcohol, petrol turpentine, disinfectant etc), burning rubber, animals or an odour associated with a place or event. When you are working with your clairscent abilities, you are essentially acting as an odor-detector who can perceive and interpret energy vibrations through your sense of smell that nobody else smells. In a mediumship sitting, you may experience distinctive smells coming through from a passed over loved one to be delivered to your sitter as information and evidence whether it is someone's favourite perfume, the smell of someone cooking a cake, cookies or specific foods, the smell from a pipe or cigarette smoke, a familiar smell from someone's workplace or home or much more. You can tune in and start developing or improving your sense of smell by playing the 'smell game' that many of you may have played as a child where you are blindfolded using a scarf, have a tray with various items on it placed directly in front of you and you are asked to use your sense of smell to identify what each item is based on the scent. For example, you may want to include various foods (cheese, coffee, cinnamon, herbs, fruit, chocolate, bananas, strawberries etc), deodorants (Rexona, Dove, Lynx, Nivea, Brut etc) and perfumes (Chanel, Gucci, Calvin Klein, Hugo etc), flowers (Carnations, Daffodil, Gerberas, Lilies, Orchids, Roses, Tulips etc) or anything else with a distinctive smell. This will allow you to start developing your sense of smell in the physical world and give you some reference points and a library of smells for those in the Spirit world to be able to bring though when they connect and communicate with you. This is a common way for mediums to receive information and is often experienced in combination with clairgustance.

CLAIRGUSTANCE

Clairgustance, 'clear tasting' allows you to be able to perceive various taste in your mouth from those in the Spirit realms, without physically having placed anything in your mouth, whether it is a substance, chemicals, medications, drugs, blood, foods, herbs, spices or other ingredients. In a mediumship sitting, you may be shown that you have a loved one in the Spirit world connecting who was a smoker so you will be given the taste of cigarettes as a way of bringing through this piece of evidence for your sitter to confirm. The use of this sense is particularly important for psychics who work with law enforcement agencies and police as it can help to provide clues whether around how a victim passed, where the person may be located, details about the scene of a crime or even information about perpetrators. Because your sense of smell and taste can work together it is important that you are conscious and aware of when you are receiving information through this way and that you work on developing these in your everyday life.

While one of your senses may be stronger or more dominant than the others, it is important not to expect Spirit to show themselves to you through this sense or for information to be delivered in the same way each time as this block the many other, and often easier, ways that spirit has available for you to receive information. So be open to communicating with and receiving information from Spirit in a variety of ways.

PRACTICAL ACTIVITIES

Firstly, to help you develop your clairvoyance, take about 30 minutes or more to go for a walk, look around, observe what is around you in your environment, what activities are going on, describe any people who are around, specifically describing their body shape, height, what clothing they are wearing, the colour and style of their hair. Also notice any sounds you may be hearing whether they are close to you or at more of a distance as well as any smells and tastes that you may be given throughout the process – you are essentially noticing everything you see, hear, feel, know, taste and smell during the time you are walking. Write down what you observed as a way of supporting your learning and development as well as reinforcing with Spirit what they will be able to bring through for you as evidence in sittings.

In addition, to develop and improve your Clairvoyance and Clairsentience, find someone you do not know personally, who has a loved one in the Spirit world to do a practice mediumship sitting with. As you set your intention and begin connecting, ask the Spirit person who is going to step forward for your sitter to give you a picture of an object or scene that is relevant for them, describe what you are seeing and then take the picture or image into your gut/stomach, recreating it and start putting what you are feeling about it into words for your sitter. Again, write down what you see and feel as a way of supporting your learning and development as well as reinforcing with Spirit what they will be able to bring through for you as evidence in future sittings.

Another activity you can do to improve your mediumship abilities is to ask someone you do not know personally to provide you with a photo of one of their loved ones who has passed over for you to blend and connect with in the Spirit world. You can then take the photo and place it in your hands, using it to connect in via psychometry and your clairsentient abilities to find out details about how the person passed, what they did for work, what they enjoyed doing in life as well as their personality and any other evidence they want to bring through for your sitter. Write down any feedback you receive from this sitting about the accuracy of the evidence as well as the ways in which the information came through from Spirit for you as a way of supporting your learning and development for future sittings.

CHAPTER 7. EXPLORING THE EVIDENCE

The reason why most people come for a mediumship reading is because they want evidence that their loved one's spirit still continues to survive after they have passed, where they are and that they are the same people they knew and loved while they were together in this world. While you and I both know that our loved ones continue to survive even after they have passed from this world, one of your responsibilities as a Medium is to provide the person in front of you, the sitter, with evidence that it is in fact their loved one you are communicating with and that you have a definite connection to them in Spirit. There are so many different types of evidence Spirit can use as evidence during a mediumship sitting, depending on their personality, style and their nature – that is who they are/were – so you must stay open to what information Spirit wants to deliver. Some mediums are good at providing information such as the person's name, addresses, telephone numbers, license plate number and other such information, which is considered great pieces of information, however, information like this may not actually prove that the person's loved one is still with them or bring any comfort or healing to the person with you having the sitting. It is also important to bring through the essence of who the person in the Spirit world REALLY was, that is their personality, likes and dislikes, what motivated them in life, memories of things they did with their loved ones while they were here. This allows the sitter to feel their loved one's presence once more, for Spirit to touch the Soul of the individual, touch their Spirit, and express "It's really me. I am here with you; I am OK". Think for a moment about if you were to pass over and then suddenly had an opportunity -- perhaps the only one -- to communicate with someone you loved, what would you want to say to them to prove and leave no doubt that it is you communicating? Let's take a look at some of the types of evidence Spirit may provide during a mediumship connection:

- **Sex or Gender Identity:** Male, Female, Androgynous (combination of male and female), Agender (not gender or gender identity), Gender-Neutral, Transgender, Transsexual etc
- **Relationship to Sitter:** Mum, Dad Grandparent, sister, brother, twin, cousin, partner, husband, wife, Aunt, Uncle, Great Grandparent, Great Uncle, Great Aunt, son, daughter, step parent, step child, adopted parent, adopted child, adopted sibling, biological parent, foster parent, foster child, organ donor, pet etc
- **Name:** First name, initial, nickname, surname, maiden name
- **Physical Appearance/Description:** Height, weight, hair type and colour, build, eye shape and colour, forehead size, shape of face, nose and/or mouth,

physical disability or impairment, physical scars, tattoos, markings, facial features, clothing, etc

- **Age:** - Specific number or an age range
- **Cause of Death/How Passed Over:** Old age, Cardiovascular/Heart disease, Heart failure, Cancer (Brain, Lung, Breast, Liver, Skin, Uterine, Bladder, Pancreatic, Cervical, Ovarian, Prostate, Mouth, Lip, Nose etc), Leukemia, Melanoma, Respiratory disease, Asthma, Stroke, Alzheimer's disease, Diabetes, Influenza, Pneumonia, SIDS, Drowning, Poisoning, Assault, Drug overdose, Parkinson's disease, Meningitis, HIV/AIDS, Accident (automobile, fall, fire, bomb, knife, medication, violence, natural disaster etc), Suicide (automobile, medication, fire, gun, knife, overdose etc), War, Murder/Homicide, Manslaughter etc
- **Marital status:** Married, widowed, separate, divorced, single, de facto, civil union, common-law marriage, cohabiting, partnership etc
- **Race/Nationality/Cultural background:** Afgan, Algerian, Argentinian, Australian, Austrian, Bangladeshi, Belgian, Brazilian, Briton, Canadian, Chilean, Chinese, Colombian, Croatian, Czech, Dane, Egyptian, English, Fijian, French, German, Greek, Dutch, Hungarian, Indian, Iranian, Iraqi, Irish, Israeli, Japanese, Kenyan, Korean, Lebanese, Malaysian, Mexican, Moroccan, Nepalese, Nigerian, Norwegian,

Pakistani, Russian, Saudi, Scottish, Spaniard, Swede, Swiss, Thai, American, Vietnamese, Zimbabwean etc

- **Work/Job/Career:** Architect, Actor/Actress, Director, Artist, Athlete, Choreographer, Coach, Writer, Designer, Engineer, Technician, Florist, Composer, Singer, Musician, Poet, Comedian, TV/Radio Presenter, Reporter, Journalist, Builder, Cleaner, Housekeeper, Landscaper, Gardener, Janitor, Maid, Pest Controller, Tree Trimmer/Lopper, Accountant, Auditor, Manager, Project/Event Manager, Financial Planner, Real Estate Agent, Banker, Training Officer, Teacher, Tutor. Professor, Educator, Retail worker, Child Care worker, Clergy, Counsellor, Guidance Officer, Marriage Therapist, Social Worker, Mental Health Specialist, Psychiatrist, Psychologist, Acupuncturist, Nurse, Doctor, Chiropractor, Dentist, Dietician, Optometrist, Surgeon, Podiatrist, Pharmacist, Speech Pathologist, Therapist, Lawyer, Judge, Firefighter, Police Officer, Detective, Correctional Officer, Paramedic, Lifeguard, Truck driver, Computer Programmer, Data Analyst, Statistician, Web Designer or Developer, Video Game Developer, Boilermaker, Carpenter, Concreter, Builder, Tiler, Electrician, Plumber, Glazier, Miner, Painter, Plasterer, Sheet Metal Worker, Farmer, Veterinarian, Barista, Bartender, Chef, Cook, Waiter/Waitress, Locksmith, Air Conditioning and Refrigeration, Mechanic, Cashier, Receptionist, Travel Agent,

Salesperson, Model, Telemarketer, Unemployed, Student etc

- **Hobbies/Sports/Interests:** Acting, baking, reading, dancing, bowling, candle making, card/board games, computing, crafts, gardening, writing, crosswords, drawing, painting, fashion, sewing designing, singing, music, fishing, flower arranging, foreign languages, soccer, netball, volleyball, running. Jogging, swimming, table tennis, baseball, cricket, camping, surfing, skate boarding, canoeing, hiking, horse riding, martial arts, photography, rock climbing, sailing, scuba diving, skiing, sky diving, travel, etc

- **Personality/Characteristics:** Out going, shy, uptight, easy going, laid back, affectionate, controlling, open, focused, anxious, moody, creative, adventurous, agreeable, articulate, appreciative, kind, warm hearted, compassionate, athletic, calm, capable, challenging, intelligent, competitive, decisive, discreet, deep, dedicated, dramatic, efficient, fun-loving, generous, honest, offensive, independent, dependent, intuitive, loyal, logical, patient, impatient, romantic, self-critical, sophisticated etc

- **Mannerisms/Habits:** walks briskly, crosses arms across chest, hands in pockets, hunched shoulders, tapping or drumming fingers, rubs eyes, biting nails, pulling or tugging ear, playing with hair, standing with hands on hips, stoking chin, clumsy, whispers, talks over people, mumbles, slurs words, talks too quickly, clears throat, whistles, hums, stutters, specific laugh, talking to self, grinding teeth, raising eyebrows, scratching head, nose twitching, licking lips. Sticking tongue out, glancing sideways, rolling or squinting eyes etc

- **Birthday:** day, date, month, year, time
- **Date of Death:** day, date, month, year, time
- **Anniversary/Special Dates:** day, date, month, year, time
- **Education level:** Primary school, High school, Certificate, Associate degree, Bachelor's degree, Honours degree, Master's degree, Doctoral degree, Professional degree etc
- **Level of Intelligence:** Extremely low, low, average, high average, superior, very superior
- **Other evidence:** Sayings, songs, music, memories, smells, lifestyle, emotional state/well-being, details about current situations in the sitter's lifeIt is important to stay open to all the potential ways in which Spirit can bring through information and for your sitter so you are delivering the clear and accurate evidence they need in order to know (beyond reasonable doubt) that their loved one is communicating with them. With all evidence you receive, make sure you explore each piece on a deeper

level by asking more questions and getting curious about it with Spirit.

It takes practice and lots of patience to learn to blend and connect with those in the Spirit world, to get out of your own way, to open to them and allow them in as well as to simply trust and flow with the information that is coming in for you to share with your sitter. It is sometimes the most trivial, seemingly insignificant or completely unknown pieces of evidence or information that are the best, as these allow the Spirit person to show their authentic selves, touch the soul of your sitter, share something that has significant personal and often private meaning for your sitter or make them go away and check or ask someone else thereby involving other loved ones in the sitting. Remember, as the loved one in the Spirit world brings through information and evidence about who they were and their life, you are providing your sitter with the opportunity to feel the presence of their loved one, for healing to take place and to bring a sense of comfort and peace as they know that their loved one is still with them. If you stick to the facts, evidence and information you are being given you will never go wrong.

CHAPTER 8. STRUCTURING THE COMMUNICATION

It is your responsibility to build trust with those in the Spirit realms by accurately and truthfully passing on each piece of information and evidence they give you, just the way they give it to you. To begin flowing with and passing on the information you are given in the moment, without doubting or judging, it is important to understand that each mediumship sitting and connection with a passed over loved one will generally be structured to move you through essentially five (5) phases. Let's take a closer look at each of these five (5) phases in a mediumship sitting and the type of information you may receive during each:

STRUCTURING THE COMMUNICATION

Essentially you can structure each communication and connection with Spirit in five (5) phases which will help you to create a strong link and build trust with the Spirit person as they draw closer and start working with you more to bring through clear, detailed and specific evidence to prove beyond reasonable doubt who they are and that the soul continues after we leave this world.

PHASE 1: INTRODUCTION

The Introduction phase is where you are building a picture or preparing your sitter for the mediumship connection by letting them know who you are, how you work, how you want them to work with you as the information comes through, by responding with only 'yes', 'no' or 'maybe' answers, asking them not to give you details about their loved one in Spirit and to let go of expectations so they are open to whoever in the Spirit world wants to step forward and communicate with them. You may want to let your sitter know at this point that you cannot guarantee communication or a connection to a specific loved one who has passed over, it is up to those in the Spirit world to step forward and that it is important to trust that the right person will step forward, at the right time with exactly the right information they need to support them in their healing process. Also, let your sitter know that you may not look directly at them or maintain eye contact with them through the sitting as well as if they will have time during the session to ask questions and to gain further information, guidance and insight from their loved one in Spirit and when they can do this. In this phase you must provide your sitter, with information about how you work, how you want them to respond or interact, address any expectations they may have and provide any other information you want them to know. Below is an example of how you might begin a mediumship sitting and the information you may provide in this phase:

"Thanks for coming to see me today for a mediumship reading. What I am going to do is call in your Guides, connect in with your energy and ask them to let me know what it is you need to know right now and what it is you need to do to move forward. The information they bring through will be exactly what you need to hear, it may not be what you want to hear so please be open to what comes through. If there is a particular area of your life that you would like guidance on, please let me know and we will make sure we cover that by the end of the reading. What I would ask you to do is just relax and give me 'yes', 'no' or 'maybe' answers if I ask, please don't give me any information. I will also give you some time towards the end of the reading to ask any additional questions or for clarification".

Take a few minutes to write down the information you will provide to your sitter about how you work, how you want them to respond or interact, how you will address possible expectations and any other information you wanted them to know at this phase.

Whatever you use for the Introduction make sure it fits with your own personality, style of reading and allows you and your sitter to feel comfortable and confident before stepping into the next phase.

PHASE 2: BLENDING

During the Blending phase the Spirit person will make the initial link with you, through your energy field and begin to draw closer, essentially allowing the essence of a loved one who has passed to the Spirit world to step into your energy. Essentially at this phase of the sitting, you are identifying who your Spirit Communicator is – in other words you are asking 'who have I got'? The connection and information you are given at this phase may not be very clear, may be quite subtle and general - for example gender, relationship and side of the family - as the Spirit person is still feeling their way around and blending with your energy. You must ensure that you are present and conscious of what is coming in through your various senses at this point as the information from the Spirit person may only be there for a second and you will need to go with it and give the information as soon as it comes in. It is important here to be brave and provide whatever information you are given as this will help you to open up, allows the Spirit person to feel more comfortable to draw closer and establish a stronger connection with you and builds trust and faith as you work together to reconnect them with their loved one having the sitting with you. Do not give up or sit in silence, verbalise what you are receiving, continue communicating with the loved one in Spirit, making sure you allow them time and the opportunity to provide you with the information you have asked for. Remember, your role here is to build and strengthen the connection so you can move to the next phase where more tangible and specific evidence or information is offered. You may experience problems in this phase such as complete silence, feeling blocked or giving up and conclude the message without offering any tangible evidence or information to your sitter to prove who you are communicating with, if you do not work to establish the strong link with your Spirit person. Below is an example of some leading sentences you might use at this phase of your sitting to help build the connection, keep the energy flowing and have the courage to pass on the initial pieces of information you are receiving from your Spirit Communicator:

"As I connect with Spirit" or "As I become aware of the Spirit world coming closer to me"

'I see_____'

'I hear_____'

'I know_____'

'I feel_____'

It is important in this phase, and throughout the entire sitting, to offer the evidence the Spirit person is providing you with as statements – not questions – and that you ensure your sitter is only responding with a 'yes', 'no' or 'maybe' to the information you are bringing through. Do not engage in conversation with the sitter, or your mind will jump in, you may start questioning whether you are getting the information psychically or through the Spirit person. Make sure that you work with your intuition and Spirit to use the appropriate leading sentences to reflect which sense you are receiving the information through and that whatever you use to help you get into the flow of bringing through the information and evidence, fits with your own style and feels right for you.

Take a few minutes to write down, what leading sentences you will use to help initially identify who the Spirit person is as well as to bring through the evidence and information they provide you with at this phase of your sitting.

PHASE 3: EVIDENCE

In the Evidence phase, the Spirit person maintains a strong connection with you, information begins flowing quickly and clearly with more specific evidence and facts are now being provided as you blend more closely. It is important at this stage that you ask questions (who, what, when, where, how, why) to the Spirit person to bring through more detailed evidence and information that will prove beyond reasonable doubt who they are. In other words, this is where your Spirit person 'proves who they are' to your sitter and brings through the real essence of who they are. The evidence you receive at this stage is more detailed, specific and deeper and may include how they passed, initials or name, their age, physical description (height, clothing, build, hair colour etc), personality (habits, humour, mannerisms), profession, study, hobbies, family/partner, nationality/cultural background, memories, what's happening in your sitter's life now etc. Remember the evidence, proof of survival, you bring through can be given subtly and very quickly, in a second, so you must be present, aware and open to all the different types of information that can come in and give the information exactly as you receive it. You do not need to interpret the information or evidence you are being given when you are doing a mediumship sitting, you just need to describe exactly what you see, hear, feel, know. smell and taste and leave what it means to the sitter. Sometimes in a mediumship connection, it is a single piece of information (that may seem insignificant to you) that is essential in connecting the person you are doing the sitting for with who you are communicating with in the Spirit world. You can continue using your sentence starters in this phase - 'As I continue to connect to Spirit', 'I see_____', 'I hear _____', 'I know _____' and 'I feel _____' as you begin asking the Spirit person questions to help you gather and bring through more detailed evidence and information to 'prove who they are'. Below are some examples of questions you might begin asking to the Spirit person in this phase:

- How did you pass over? or What was the cause of your passing?
- What age were you when you passed? or What month did you pass over?

133

- When was your birthday? or Were there any dates that were important to you?

- Where were you born? or What is your cultural background? or Where did you live?

- What did you do for work? or What was your occupation? or How did they feel about their job?

- Were there any sports you played? or Were there any hobbies you enjoyed? or Was there something that you had an interest in or were passionate about?

- How would you describe your personality? or Were there any characteristics that made you different from other people?

- Were there any scars or unusual markings on your body? or Did you have any tattoos?

The possibilities with the questions you can ask the Spirit person are endless. So, make sure you work with them closely, be inquisitive and ask for as much information as you can about who they were and how they lived their life – they had a life just like you, so find out about them in a way that feels right for you. It is also essential in this phase that you remain in 'control' of the link with the Spirit person you are blending and connecting with by ensuring that you deliver the evidence as a statement of fact not as a question as well as making sure your sitter only provides you with 'yes', 'no' or 'maybe' responses to each piece of evidence you are bringing through. If you receive a 'maybe' from your sitter, simply go back to the Spirit person and ask them to clarify, re-word or give you more information about the evidence that they are wanting to pass on and communicate. If you receive a 'no' from your sitter, don't panic. This is simply an opportunity for you to go back to Spirit and check that your evidence is correct by going back to the last piece of evidence you gave where you received a 'yes' from your sitter and getting back into the flow with the information and trusting what is being brought through. If your sitter is still giving you a 'no', you may need to go back and get confirmation that you are still with the same Spirit person as you may have had another Spirit person step in wanting to communicate so you will need to go back to phase 2 and find out who it is you have got then move back into this phase with the next Spirit person. Once the Spirit person feels satisfied with the communication, that your sitter knows exactly who they are and that they have brought through the essence of who they were when they were in the physical world, the Spirit person will move into the next phase.

Take a few minutes to write down, the questions you may ask the Spirit person to provide answers to as well as the specific and detailed evidence that may be provided when you communicate and connect in this phase that prove beyond reasonable doubt who they are to your sitter.

PHASE 4: WRAP-UP

During the Wrap-Up phase, the Spirit person starts bringing through information to explain more about the reason they are connecting or the message they want to pass on to their loved one, your sitter, in other words they will identify 'why have they come'. The information at this stage may include help and support for your sitter with situations, problems or difficulties they may be experiencing in their life, guidance and help with decision making, tools and strategies to help them move forward or simply bringing through healing, encouragement, inspiration and their love. Once you have delivered the message of why the Spirit person has come to their loved one, you can ask if they have any final questions they would like to ask before you finish the sitting. Once they have shared what they wanted to say or pass on, then you will feel their energy start to withdraw and pull back, becoming less clear with the connection gradually weakening as your energy fields separate and they step out completely for you to bring the sitting to a close.

Take some time to write down, the reason(s) why the Spirit person may want to connect and communicate with their loved one, your sitter, what their message might be as well as how you will know when to wrap-up the sitting.

PHASE 5: CONCLUSION

In the Conclusion phase, you may want to thank your sitter for their time, let them know that their loved ones are around them and to offer any other closing statement that feels right for you. Below is an example of what you might say at this phase to finish your sitting:

Thank you so much for working with me and allowing me to connect in with your energy to bring you through guidance to support you and help you move forward in your everyday life.

Take some time to write down, how you will thank your sitter for coming, the information you might provide them to let them know that their loved one is still around as well as what information or closing statement you will give to finish your sitting.

While moving through each of these phases it is important to remember that it is an interactive process, like you are having a conversation with a person you have just met, to get the information you want, you have to ask for it – so, you need to ask questions to the Spirit person throughout the entire sitting and you will continue to receive answers (visual, thoughts, feel, sound, taste, smell etc). When Spirit gives you the answer, you must give exactly what they give you, don't miss anything, skip information, linger on it, hold onto it, repeat it, create a story around it, analyse it, think about what it might mean.....just give it and move on. Be aware of what you are saying and how you are saying it, your voice, tone and mannerisms during the sitting as this may also be evidence from the Spirit person that is important for your sitter too.

PRACTICAL ACTIVITY

Now that you have an understanding of how to structure a mediumship sitting and each of the phases you will move through to connect and communication with a loved one in Spirit, find a volunteer who is willing to allow you to do a practice sitting for them where you will flow through each of the phases and gather information as outlined above. Then write down what information you provided to your sitter throughout each of the five (5) phases as well as any feedback you received about the accuracy and style of communication in your mediumship sitting.

CHAPTER 9. DELIVERING THE COMMUNICATION

Once Spirit connects and blends with your energy, it is your responsibility to deliver the information and evidence they are providing you to prove beyond reasonable doubt who they are to your sitter. Like any form of communication, it is an active two-way process that involves asking questions and being open to receiving the evidence and information that comes through as a result, so you are able to easily and quickly deliver what you are being given to your sitter. When you deliver this evidence in your mediumship sittings, you are being asked to trust and have faith that what is coming through is exactly what you are being asked to deliver and to have the confidence to take the risk of getting it wrong. To some of you this will come naturally and you will find it is easy to place your logical mind to one side, quieten your thoughts, get out of your own way and simply allow the information Spirit is providing to flow through you. For others, you may come across blocks to communication which are created by fear of seeing, hearing or sensing Spirit, getting the information wrong or doubts about your own abilities or the information you are being given. This can make the process of communicating with Spirit more challenging and difficult, creating noise and blocking you from connecting and communicating with Spirit. Let's explore some of the ways in which you can block connection and communication with Spirit in your mediumship sittings and how you can step into trust and flow with the information those in the Spirit world bring through to get the evidence and message across in the best way possible.

BLOCKS TO COMMUNICATION

PREPARING INFORMATION

Many problems in mediumship sittings are caused by the Medium feeling as if they need to have a complete connection with information, facts, evidence and the message formulated within the mind before starting. It is important that you remember, the only way you can prepare for a mediumship sitting is to sit with Spirit and let them know you are ready to connect and blend with them, you cannot prepare or formulate the information before hand, it must be spontaneous and done in the moment or your logical mind can get in the way of what the Spirit person is asking you to pass on. Each mediumship sitting will be different, you will never know what type of evidence and information will come through, how it will be delivered to you or what message will come through for your sitter until you open your mouth and begin speaking. The best connections often come through when you let go of expectations, which requires a level of courage to open up and be vulnerable as well as trust and faith in yourself, your Spirit Team and the Spirit person you are connecting and blending with – remember Spirit will never let you down.

DOUBT

Doubt, "a feeling of uncertainty about the truth" (Webster's dictionary), can immediately block communication from Spirit to a lesser or greater extent depending on your own energy, the Spirit person, the sitter, circumstances and conditions the Mediumship sitting is taking place. Doubt can appear in many forms whether you question your abilities, feel confused or uncertain about the information being given to you, reach for the answers, create long scenarios or stories or you have a negative thought ('don't say anything; they will think you are an idiot' 'who are you to think you can do this'. 'what if I'm wrong' or 'I'm not worthy'). Because your brain is only capable of focusing on one thing at a time, when you have a negative thought, you immediately put up a wall and block out positive thoughts from coming into your mind or awareness. You can become more conscious of when you have slipped into doubt or negative thinking by slowing down, being present in the moment, catching the word "but" and replacing it with "and" as well as replacing negative thoughts with more positive ones. Also, if you notice yourself delivering information in long scenarios and recounting information in detail or telling stories and reaching for what something means, you are doubting the information you are receiving. When you slip into doubt you will also be using a lot more time and energy, working harder to bring through the connection and have to get back into your heart space, re-establish your connection before you begin connecting and communicating with Spirit again. All of these doubts simply come from what many refer to as the 'ego', which is playing it's role to help keep you safe and protected, like a Rottweiler dog, barking and snarling at you, keeping you frozen with fear and not taking a chance, or a Terrier that is tenacious, constantly yapping, never letting you have a moment of peace). However, when it comes to your mediumship struggling, overthinking, questioning or slipping into doubt, creates noise between you and those in Spirit, so it is essential that you become aware of what is happening, lock your ego away while you are conducting a sitting. The best way to step your ego out of the way and stop it from creating noise, is to use the tools and techniques you have available for grounding, cleansing and centering your energy so you can start overcoming your doubts, building your confidence and be able to step forward and grow with Spirit.

JUDGEMENT

When you step into judgement of yourself or another person, situation or experience you separate yourself from your authentic self and in turn from Spirit. One of the biggest things that creates fear, anxiety, doubt, blockages and noise in your ability to connect and blend with Spirit is self-judgement, which is really just about the painful stories, limiting beliefs and negative thoughts that you have about yourself that result in you comparing yourself to someone else and feeling wrong, bad, less than, unvalued, unloved or unworthy. When you step into criticising and judging yourself, what you are doing is attempting to protect yourself from failure, rejection or abandonment which leaves you feeling very anxious, stuck and miserable because you freeze and do not take appropriate actions or step out of your comfort zone. The best way to overcome any noise created by self-judgement is to become more conscious and present to the stories that you are telling yourself, then asking yourself if what you are telling yourself is true or what you want to become your truth. Once you have done that you can begin creating a new story that is more joyful, contains positive and uplifting thoughts and empowers you to move forward as well as embrace more compassion and kindness for yourself. Also, if there are any areas in your life where you have strong opinions about what is right or wrong, good or bad, for example religion, marriage, children, suicide etc, then these too can have an impact on your connection with Spirit and limit you from all of the possibilities of what can come through for you. It is important that you open up as much as you can to everyone and everything in alignment with the Divine and remember we are all ONE in Spirit's eyes. Do not project your own judgements onto others and remember that you are uniquely and perfectly you – so do not compare yourself to others.

DEALING WITH NO'S

As you begin to do more readings with different sitters, you will also need to learn how to deal with "No's" as they can provide you with a fantastic opportunity to check where you received the information from (Spirit communicator, the sitter or your logical mind), ask for clarity, stay with it, dig deeper, move on, leave it with the sitter to look into later or acknowledge that you got it wrong. It also provides an important opportunity to learn how your evidence feels, when to trust the information you are being given, to work on shifting through any doubts and to strengthen your connection. Remember, a mediumship sitting is a two-way interactive communication process, so go back to Spirit and tell them you need more information or clarity about the piece of evidence you received a 'no' for. For example, tell Spirit 'that's too general give me something more' or 'I'm not sure, can you give me something else'. If you go back and check the information and you realise you brought it through in the wrong way, let the sitter know and correct it or simply move on to another piece of evidence if needed. You can also get back in your flow by going back to the evidence of most significance and go deeper with it or to the last piece of evidence that you received a 'yes' from the sitter for and continue from there.

LINGERING OR HOLDING ON

While it is important to make sure you explore each piece of evidence you receive on a deeper level by asking more questions and getting curious about it, you must know when to move onto the next piece of information Spirit wants to pass on. If you are receiving 'yes' answers from your sitter and then suddenly start getting 'no's' you may be holding onto a piece of evidence and trying to stretch the information out, so it is time to let it go and move on to something else or go to the message. So, don't block the communication by holding on, the sooner you get back to delivering information that gives you a 'yes' answer from your sitting the better, as this will increase your confidence and allow Spirit to bring through more.

FEAR

Fear is an unpleasant often strong emotion caused by anticipation or awareness of danger (Merriam-Webster, 2019) which creates obstacles, problems, difficulties and resistance not only in your everyday life but also in your mediumship as it can block you from receiving information from the Spirit world clearly and accurately. In your mediumship fear can present itself in a variety of ways, whether you get defensive, worry about being judged, feel insecure or like you are not good enough, have high expectations of self, others or Spirit, seek acceptance or approval, want to avoid rejection, hide who you are and what you can do or as misconceptions about Spirit. For those stepping into your mediumship, there may have been or can be a fear of seeing, hearing or sensing Spirit which can also block you from moving forward with your mediumship development. It is important for you to understand that you are always in control of who or what comes into your energy field, you have the power to give or deny permission for Spirit to connect with you, to create boundaries around how you want to work with them and around what you are comfortable and uncomfortable with seeing, hearing and feeling. One of the best ways to begin reducing a fear of the Spirit world, is by educating, informing and preparing yourself so you can quickly become more in control of HOW and WHEN you receive information, so you are not surprised and are consciously aware of what is happening. If you are seeing, hearing or sensing too much, you have more than likely forgotten you are in control, you may be fearful of telling Spirit you are not comfortable, forgotten you can ask them to make their energy less intense, are scared to speak up and tell them to get out of your space and have not consciously set boundaries with your Spirit Team around when and how Spirit people can connect and blend with you. Talk to your Guides and let them know you are not comfortable, ask them to turn it down, slow things down and give it to you at a pace you are more comfortable with. You can also ask for things to be turned up, to be made clearer, less intense, tune them out completely, ignore them, tell them to go away etc. To conquer your fear, you must be brave and learn to trust that the reason you see and feel these things is because you have a GIFT for doing so – remember not everyone is able to connect and communicate with those in the Spirit world. Ask your fear to step aside before you connect in and then simply allow those in the Spirit world to blend with you more easily and bring through quality evidence and information for the person you are conducting the sitting for. While you always have the power to give or deny permission for Spirit to connect with you, if you ever get into a position where you do not feel like you can control what you are seeing, hearing or sensing, ask someone to help you transform what you are experiencing and get support with setting boundaries - you don't have to deal with it on your own – ask for help and support. Most importantly, one of the best ways to transform your fear into confidence is to communicate with Spirit more often as it becomes easier to step out of your own way and establish a stronger connection, trust the information you are being given.

DELIVERING EFFECTIVE COMMUNICATION

To deliver the communication from those in the Spirit world during a mediumship sitting effectively, you must remember that it is an active two-way process of asking questions, being open to receiving the answers, trusting and flowing with what you are receiving as well as using appropriate words, body language and tone of voice. You may also need to use empathy and compassion as you support your sitter through any emotions or thoughts that come up as a result of connecting with their passed over loved one during the mediumship connection by being conscious of your words, body language, tone of voice as well as using active listening skills.

COMMUNICATION SKILLS

Basic communication skills are important to develop and improve in your physical world as they will also help you to deliver the information and evidence given in a mediumship sitting more effectively and clearly. This then helps you to stay in the flow with Spirit, trust and have confidence in what they are giving you, as you move through each of the phases in delivering your communication, continue speaking and giving the information, with your sitter validating the evidence throughout the sitting. To deliver the information and evidence you receive from those in the Spirit world confidently and effectively, it is essential you have good communication skills including being aware of the words you use, your tone of voice, body language and expressions as well as active listening and empathy skills.

WORDS

Each and every day you use thousands of words with people, whether your husband, wife, partner, family, friends, clients or colleagues, which make up only about 8% of the message you are wanting to communicate and get across. Words can have a significant impact on our communication with others and with Spirit. When connecting to those in the Spirit world, it is important to actively ask questions and for information to be brought through to confirm that you can pass on to your sitter so they know beyond reasonable doubt you are bringing through their passed over loved one. To do this effectively you must ask the Spirit person only one question at a time, keep them short, simple and specific, like a Google Search – the more direct and clear the question, the easier and quicker the information will come through. When you deliver the evidence those in Spirit are giving you in response to your question, you must communicate this honestly and using the exact words and in the exact way they have given it to you one piece of evidence at a time. Be aware of the words you are using during your mediumship connections as these may be more significant for your sitter than you realise. For example, you may find yourself saying something word-for-word that the Spirit person said to their loved one just before they passed, you may start using phases or words that you normally do not use, find yourself using metaphors as part of the evidence that they want you to communicate and pass on. The words people say in their everyday life and pass on during a mediumship sitting can demonstrate a lot about their personality and style of communication and has a profound and lasting impact.

BODY LANGUAGE

It is important to be aware of your body language, not only because it accounts for approximately 55% of the communication that you as the Medium deliver to your sitter, but also because those in the Spirit world also may work through your clairsentience abilities and have you moving your body in similar ways that they did when they were still in the physical world. For example, if you are tired, slumped in your chair, your facial expressions demonstrate that you are stressed, not present, uninterested in being there and want to be somewhere else then your sitter will not take in the majority of the information and evidence that their loved one from the Spirit world is bringing through. Alternatively, you may notice throughout the sitting that your body language shifts and changes significantly whether through your posture, facial expressions, gestures or movements you are making with your hands, arms or legs, this may be Spirit blending and connecting with you and wanting you to express what you are receiving from them to your sitter for acknowledgement – once confirmed this will tend to shift back to your normal body language.

TONE OF VOICE

Your tone of voice is also important to consider when you are delivering information from Spirit. For example, a low pitch may indicate you are connecting with a male as they tend to have deeper voices or a person who is authoritative and knowledgeable or a high pitch would generally indicate you are connecting with a female or someone who is smaller in statue and generally more submissive. Also, be aware of the volume you are using, if you are bringing through information in a soft and gentle way, this may indicate that you have a passed loved one who was a more quietly spoken person in the way they communicated or that the person lacked confidence, was shy or timid. Alternatively, if you begin communicating at a higher volume and speaking more loudly, you may be connecting and communicating with a passed loved one who enjoyed being the centre of attention, liked being heard or someone who was more aggressive in their communication with others. You may also notice during a mediumship sitting that you start using different tones for different words, this is usually the passed over loved one showing where the emphasis needs to be placed, conveying their passion, enthusiasm and excitement and to add meaning to what they are asking you to pass on to your sitter. Also, be aware of the pace you are bringing through the information from the loved one in Spirit as this can also show information about the personality of the person you are connecting with and help the sitter to integrate the message that is being brought through for them.

ACTIVE LISTENING

Active Listening is an extremely important skill to be able to utilise in mediumship sessions, as it is your responsibility to give your full, undivided, attention and presence to not only those in the Spirit world as you blend and connect in but also to your sitter throughout their time with you. This is a key skill required by counsellors and therapists that is important for you to begin to develop, as it involves you reflecting back the words, feelings and information you believe the other person is expressing and experiencing and to then be able to check in that you have understood the communication correctly. In a mediumship sitting, you are essentially using your active listening skills as you connect and blend with the passed over loved ones in the Spirit world and to reflect the words, feelings and evidence they are giving you exactly as you receive it to your sitter. You may also find that during a connection to a passed over loved one, any unresolved or unexpressed grief, anger, hurt or sadness can come to the surface to be expressed and communicated, so it is important to be able to use your active listening skills to support your sitter and help them to feel comfortable and relaxed to embrace the opportunity for healing, peace and love through their connecting to those in the Spirit world. Remember, during your mediumship connection to stay connected to the energy of those in the Spirit realms and not to drop into the energy of your sitter as this is not a counselling or therapy session and most of you will not be qualified to step into this space. You can demonstrate that you understand what they are feeling or their emotional state by expressing compassion and empathy for them, however, it is not your role to take on their emotions, you must honour and respect their healing process by allowing them to experience their emotions. It is also your responsibility to respect, honour and look after the well-being of your sitter, so if you feel they need additional help and support to move through their grief, loss and emotions, please ensure you refer them to an appropriately qualified professional.

TRUST AND STAYING IN FLOW

To connect and blend with Spirit effectively there must be a level of trust and a cooperative relationship between you and the person in Spirit. Like relationships in the physical world, you must establish a solid foundation of trust which takes confidence, practice and patience on your part with your Guides in order to connect and blend with Spirit. Once Spirit blends with your energy and steps in closer to begin working with you, it is your responsibility to build trust with them by accurately and truthfully passing on each piece of information they give you, just the way they give it to you. The more you practice blending and connecting with Spirit, the more confident you will become in recognising and understanding when your energy changes and a passed over loved one steps close to communicate. Once you begin receiving information and passing what you are given on to your sitter, without doubting or judgement, the Spirit person will begin to draw closer to you and start working with you more because you have demonstrated you are capable of being trusted. Some of you may find that it is easy to place your logical mind to one side and to simply allow the information to flow through you, the more you practice sitting in the flow with Spirit, moving with them, continuing to speak and give the information, the more confident you will become and the more validations you will receive from your sitter about the evidence you are bringing through from their loved one. You have the capability to deliver accurate, professional and effective mediumship connections with loved ones who have passed over, it is simply a matter of getting into a regular practice and discipline of sitting with the power of Spirit, connecting with the silence within and moving the logic mind out of the way to allow those in the Spirit world to support you in your learning and growth as well as communicate with you and their loved ones in the physical world. Remember, it can take practice to learn to get out of your own way so that the true information can simply flow through you – so relax and imagine that the answers are right in front of you, you only need to open them and allow them in. If you stick to the facts, evidence and information you are being given you will never go wrong.

PRACTICAL ACTIVITIES

You now have a better understanding of how fear, doubt, judgements and noise can have an impact on your ability to develop an effective mediumship sitting from those in the Spirit world to your sitter. Take some time to write down, any fears you may have about working with those in the Spirit world as well as any physical, mental, emotional and spiritual boundaries you may want to establish around what you are comfortable and uncomfortable connecting to.

Also take a few minutes to write down the ways in which your doubt is experienced physically, mentally, emotionally and spiritually before, during or after a mediumship connection, how this creates noise between you and Spirit and you and your sitter as well as any strategies you will put in place to deal with receiving a 'no' to information you bring through in a sitting.

Now that you have an understanding of the importance of trust and flow in delivering an effective and professional mediumship sitting, take a few minutes to write down what trust looks like, sounds like and feels like for you and the strategies you intend to put in place to help you stay in the flow with Spirit.

CHAPTER 10. ONGOING DEVELOPMENT

Whether you are interested in learning about mediumship for fun, for your personal growth or to connect and work with Spirit on a part-time or full-time basis by delivering sittings to others, it is important to remember it is an ongoing process of development that you need to consciously choose to engage in. In continuing your learning and development journey, you may wish to think about some of the following ongoing development resources and opportunities, depending on what feels right for you.

CONNECT WITH YOUR SPIRIT GUIDES

As you know each member of your Main Spirit Team includes a team of be-ings in the Spirit realms who have been assigned exclusively to you in order to inspire, guide, teach, make you laugh, help you listen, resolve problems, comfort you, help with decisions, provide encouragement, support you, love you and help you to follow your passion. Because it is a two-way relationship, you require those in the Spirit world and passed over loved ones to work with you to bring through the information and evidence in clear, accurate and easy ways for you to deliver to the person having a mediumship sitting. To do this, it is essential that you show-up for Spirit and you commit to working with your Guides on a regular basis, check in on the role they are playing in your personal and spiritual development, understand your strengths and weaknesses, strengthen the relationship, build trust, improve your communication, reinforce or adjust your boundaries, know how they think, act and feel as well as to seek guidance and insight to help you in your everyday life.

The best way to strengthen and build the relationship with your guides is to simply take the time to sit in meditation with each of them, be present with them, connect and communicate with them as if they were a normal part of your everyday life. In doing this be flexible and learn to adopt your method and style of communication, way of thinking and acting depending on which Guide you are working with so you establish a system which works most effectively for both of you. If you are experiencing challenges or problems, whether within your everyday life or with you mediumship connections, make an appointment to sit with them and ask for their assistance, feedback and guidance about how you can resolve it or work on developing your abilities in a certain area. Communicating, connecting and working with your Spirit Guides is an on-going process, which takes time, dedication, commitment, effort, encouragement, flexibility and most of all patience, like any relationship. Please make sure you also record and write down the information and guidance you receive whether for yourself or you pass on to others as this helps you to be able to ground your processes, evaluate the quality of the information as well as gain validation of the accuracy and relevance for yourself or the person sitting for you, which will increase your confidence and help you learn and grow.

PERSONAL DEVELOPMENT

While spiritual development includes understanding that you are a soul in a physical body and always connected with and have a relationship with the wider universal force, that is 'Spirit', 'Source', 'Universe', 'God', 'Buddha', 'Mohammed' or whatever you refer to it as, personal development is not necessarily spiritual. Personal Development is an essential aspect of your spiritual development as they work hand-in-hand and presents you with an opportunity to regularly improve your life mentally, physically and spiritually as well as to experience new things to help you grow as a person. In developing personally, you are asked to be open to learning and growing as an individual, healing and shifting through fears, old patterns and beliefs, becoming more consciously aware and present to your thoughts, emotions and actions in your everyday life as well as letting go of anything that may be holding you back and reflecting on your experiences to gain the wisdom and understanding so you improve your ability to connect to the Spirit realms. There are a variety of ways in which you can grow personally, whether taking on a new hobby, learning a new skill, learning to manage your daily tasks more effectively, techniques for becoming more productive, time management and coping with stress, mindfulness and relaxation or keeping up to date in your professional life. Essentially personal development is linked to anything that supports you in growing and being more effective in your everyday life and can often result in drastic changes in how you think and perceive the world around you as well as in your career path, relationships, with family, friends and co-workers, health and well-being as well as your spiritual development. It's a 'lifelong process' and a commitment regularly working on improving yourself as a person, by prioritising yourself, building and strengthening your relationships with others, assessing natural skills and abilities as well as identifying and focusing on your goals and dreams in life. This process can be sometimes challenging and difficult, however, with perseverance it can provide you with the key to well-being and success in various areas of your life.

DEVELOPMENT CIRCLES

As you know, developing your mediumship requires commitment, dedication and consistency and one of the best ways to ensure you put in the time and energy to your own development and to turn up for Spirit to work with you is to join a development circle hosted by an experienced working medium. These circles, historically referred to as a séance, are typically made up of between 8-15 people who as a group come together with the intention to develop themselves personally and spiritually. While each medium will work differently, most circles will typically last between 1 to 2 hours and usually follows a format that includes a meditation to lift your vibration ready to connect and give you an opportunity to gain knowledge and insights about how the Spirit world works, ask for advice and guidance as well as practice connecting, blending and communicating with the Spirit world to deliver messages through your various senses to strangers in a safe and supportive environment intended to help you learn and grow. Attending a regular Development Circle is a fantastic way to not only lift your vibration and connect with Spirit, they provide you with the opportunity to create discipline in your work, connect with like-minded people who are interested in developing their mediumship, share experiences and gain support from others, practice giving sittings to others and being able to instantly gain feedback on the accuracy of the messages you provide. As these groups tend to be held in local areas with like-minded people, they provide the perfect space to develop your skills, try new approaches and exchange information. If you are unable to find a circle in your local area contact a psychic or medium close by or look into some other online meditation or development groups which have started to become available for people to access from the comfort of their own home. Development circles are one of the best spaces for a medium who is wanting to learn, grow and develop.

Read Books

One of the best ways to continue your spiritual development is to read books as they allow you to expand your awareness, improve your mindset, provoke new ideas, open you to new processes and techniques as well as help you see the world differently. Allowing yourself to take time out from do-ing to simply be and immerse yourself in a good book is uplifting for the soul, improves your focus and concentration, increases your memory, provides mental stimulation (great for an active mind), expands your knowledge base, opens you to additional wisdom and insights as well as being a fantastic way to relax, reduce stress and embrace peace and stillness in your life. There are a vast array of quality books available whether in print form or as ebooks you can access anywhere and anytime to suit you, ask your Teacher Guide to support you and draw you to the books that are in your highest and greatest good and will benefit you in your personal and mediumship development.

Private Sittings

The best way to continue your mediumship development is by Conducting Private Sittings with people you do not know and to start blending and connecting with loved ones who have passed over as they will help and support you in your learning and help you develop new awareness and insights into the different types of information and evidence that can be delivered. While some of you may find that you are more comfortable doing sittings for members of your family or close friends, however, it is important to remember that mediumship is about proving beyond reasonable doubt that life continues after we leave this physical world. When you are connecting and blending with a loved one in Spirit who you already know, you are not really honouring the purpose of mediumship and not allowing your family and close friends to have the experience of a connection with your loved one from someone who knows nothing about the passed loved one. You may also find it easier to allow your logical brain to step to the side and to trust the information and evidence those in the Spirit world want you to deliver when you are doing a sitting for someone you have no background knowledge about their loved ones, life situation, experiences or circumstances. It takes time, understanding and practice to have confidence in conducting a private sitting for people you do not know and to trust the information so you can begin to gain validation of the accuracy of what you are delivering to your sitter, which helps you to fine-tune and improve your skills to deliver accurate and professional mediumship connections. If you are just starting out with conducting mediumship connections for others, keep them short, 5-10 minutes and as you increase your confidence increase the amount of time to 30 minutes or 1 hour depending on the depth of the connection to the Spirit realms, the information and evidence being brought through for the person having the sitting. As you continue to practice and bring through evidence from passed over loved ones, you will learn to understand how to explain what you see, hear, feel, know, taste and smell, it is an ongoing practice, so experiment with various methods and ways of bringing through the information to find what works best for you and the style of medium you wish to be.

MENTORING OR COACHING

Another fantastic way to continue your mediumship development is to find a Mentor or Coach, that is a person who can guide you, support you and help you in the process of gathering knowledge, wisdom, understanding, share various skills, techniques and strategies with you as well as support you in developing abilities and encourage you to successfully achieve your goals. The role of a mentor or coach is to not only share information and understanding with you, it is also to inspire, encourage and support you to take your personal, intuitive, and mediumship abilities to the next level while receiving help, tools and techniques to refine your skills as well as practical experiences with conducting sittings for others to increase your confidence, connection and trust with delivering information from those in Spirit in ways that are easy and best suited to your personality and how you enjoy being in the world. Once again, there are a variety of methods that Mentors and Coaches will offer to support you in your development, whether through in-person, phone or online sessions, courses, workshops, group or individual programs and retreats. It is essential that when you are looking for a Mentor or Coach you consider what your specific goals and intentions are with your development, their qualifications, professional and personal background as well as their level of expertise and experience. Remember, this is about your on-going development, be prepared to invest in yourself, in your abilities and in improving your connection with those in the Spirit realms and they will also invest in and support you. If you are interested in learning more through any of my spiritual development or one-on-one coaching programs, further details are available from www.thebarefootmedium.com.au.

OTHER BOOKS BY LEANNE, THE BAREFOOT MEDIUM®

Psychic Development: Basics of Working with Spirit

This book provides an in-depth understanding of the fundamental skills and techniques necessary to begin working with energy and Spirit. It is filled with practical easy to follow strategies to help you to build a solid foundation and have all the tools necessary to understand how you can enhance your physical health, emotional balance and mental well-being to work more closely with your intuition in your everyday life as well as in your psychic and mediumship work.

Psychic Development: Divination Tools and Techniques

This book provides easy and practical techniques to help you understand more about your intuition, different tools that can be used for divination as well as understand how information is communicated through the various senses. It includes step-by-step processes and activities to help you connect with your Spirit Guides, perceive and read information within the aura and chakra's as well as how to work with different divination tools such as tarot cards, pendulums and automatic writing for guidance into situations, events, relationships and possible opportunities for the future.

ONE LAST THING...

If you enjoyed this book or found it useful, I would be very grateful if you can take a few moments to post a short review on Amazon. Your support really does make a difference and I read all the reviews personally so I can get your feedback and make this book even better.

If you'd like to leave a review then all you need to do is click the review link on this book's page on Amazon.

As a thank you for your support, I would love to invite you to kick off your shoes and join me in the **Barefoot Tribe** where you will receive channeled guidance from Spirit, gifts and more to support you on your journey. When you sign up you will also be the first to receive new episodes of Barefoot with Spirit podcast shows, details about up-coming webinars, events, masterclasses as well as early release and pre-sale on my products, services & offerings!

Sign-up via my website and I look forward to seeing you in the Tribe! Just remember ... **Shoes are absolutely optional!**

www.thebarefootmedium.com.au.

www.ingramcontent.com/pod-product-compliance
Lightning Source LLC
Chambersburg PA
CBHW072142090426
42739CB00013B/3265